# SUSHI

## MASUO YOSHINO

Published by GAKKEN CO., LTD.
4-40-5 Kami-ikedai, Ohta-ku, Tokyo 145-8502, Japan

First edition 1986
Second edition 1990
Eighth printing 1999
ISBN: 0-87040-742-2
ISBN: 4-05-151404-8 (in Japan)
Printed in Japan

**Credits:**

**Sushi Makers**
—"The World of Sushi" & "The Joy of Sushi"—
Sushi shop "Yoshino-Zushi-Honten"
Masuo Yoshino
Shōjirō Yoshino
Mitsuo Uchida
Kazuhiro Ōsawa
—"The Pleasure of Sushi-Making"—
Etsuko Ogiwara
—Sushi in The Kansai District in "The World of Sushi"—
Sushi shop "Kodai-Suzume-Zushi Sushiman"
Sushi shop "Kyoto Izuu"
Sushi shop "Osaka Takotake"
Sushi shop "Osaka Yoshino-Zushi"

**Sushiware**
Japanese lacquerware shop "Yamagataya-Shikki-Ten"

**Book Design**
Gow Michiyoshi
Kazuyo Nakamura

**Photography**
Masaya Suzuki

**Co-Editor**
Yoshiko Okano

# Preface

This book is a kind of guidebook to sushi, mainly hand-formed sushi (*nigiri*-zushi). This is intended not only to afford the people of the world a better understanding of what sushi is but also to enjoy eating and making sushi more through a more in-depth understanding of sushi.

Hand-formed sushi has developed to a remarkable extent especially over the last 40 or so years. Originally, hand-formed sushi was food for Tokyoites, but today it is eaten widely throughout Japan, and in areas where fresh fish and shellfish can be obtained to a plentiful extent, delicious hand-formed sushi which is not available on the counters of sushi shops in Tokyo is made and offered.

Moreover, hand-formed sushi is enjoyed in all parts of the world. It is only natural that it should become popular in parts of the world where good rice, proper *tane* and high quality brewed vinegar are available and where people have or can learn the art of sushi-making.

Nothing gives more joy to us engaged in the sushi-making business than to find that sushi is being enjoyed by people the world over. However, at the same time, we cannot overlook the fact that there are a lot of wrong ideas and information about sushi circulating in the world. Incorrect information would greatly damage the reputation of sushi.

Let us take a simple example to demonstrate how hand-formed sushi is formed. Some people may have the wrong idea about it and think that sushi is no more than a ball of rice topped with *tane*. However, a hand-formed sushi differs entirely from that of a canapé. It could be better compared to a sandwich which is made by after inserting eatables between two pieces of bread and then pressing them.

It is only when sushi is formed in such a way that sushi rice is able to stick to *tane* properly that the fermented taste can be instantly given to sushi. This is the reason that such sushi whose *tane* falls apart before reaching one's mouth, is found lacking in taste.

But surprisingly, there is a lot of sushi being made which crumbles before it can be eaten! If this type of sushi were to be accepted as sushi worldwide, how extremely unfortunate it would be for those who enjoy and relish sushi. I would like to have you understand that the sushi-forming skill is very important and that the taste of sushi depends on how well it is formed.

In addition, there is a lot of wrong information being circulated as if it were authoritative information about the origins and history of sushi and also about how to eat sushi properly.

For instance, it is said that you should begin with omelet sushi in eating sushi and that you should eat sushi according to very defined and set manners. Furthermore, it is said that it is only second-rate and third-rate sushi shops that serve powdered horseradish. These ideas are wrong and are no longer considered valid today.

For more detailed information about these matters, I would like you to refer to this book. At any rate, there are quite a few people who still believe in these and other wrong ideas.

I have, for a great many years, collected books and documents on sushi, my library now covering everything concerning sushi with articles and books numbering in the thousands. I have studied all the materials carefully and when a question should arise, I would direct my inquiry to an expert in that particular field.

For example, when I heard that the Iban tribe (so-called head-hunters) in North Borneo eat something like fermented sushi, which they call "*Kassam*", I asked to be included in a research team as a member in 1984 and had the great opportunity of going there and tasting this variety.

Needless to say, as a proprietor of a sushi shop, I have been making sushi for a long time and have heard a great many stories about sushi from my parents when they were alive.

This book is the sum total of what I have studied and experienced. Due to the limited space of this book, it was impossible to tell all here, but I am sure that I have touched upon the main points, and I hope both sushi-eaters and sushi-makers will be satisfied with the content of this book.

In passing, let me remark on the relation between hand-formed sushi and vinegar.

Vinegar plays an important role in making various kinds of sushi, including hand-formed sushi. If it had not been for brewed vinegar, there would not be any hand-formed sushi as we know it today.

Allow me to be a bit academic. With the use of vinegar, rice is fermented in a short time because, it is believed that considerable amounts of acetic acid and lactic acid exist in vinegar and succinic acid is the flavoring component of Japanese rice wine (*sake*), constituting the taste of sushi, if viewed from a biochemical standpoint.

If you want to make good-tasting sushi, you cannot be too particular about the vinegar you use. My father was extremely insistent on this point.

Lastly, I would like to publicly thank Ms. Etsuko Ogiwara and Ms. Akiko Sugawara, who kindly wrote two sections on "The Pleasure of Sushi-Making" and "Sushi and Health", respectively, from their standpoint as specialists.

吉野昇雄

Masuo Yoshino

At Nihonbashi 3-chome,
Tokyo, August 1986

# CONTENTS

# The Pleasure of Sushi-Making

# How to Use This Book

There are a lot of variations in sushi-making—in the preparation of materials, sushi-forming and seasoning, and there is no firmly established ways for the making of sushi. Each sushi shop has developed its own unique ways of making sushi. However, at the same time, there are traditional work methods peculiar to sushi shops. In this sense, the art of sushi-making explained in Chapter 1 "The World of Sushi" and Chapter 2 "The Joy of *Nigiri*-Zushi" follows the ways of sushi-making jealously guarded by those well-known sushi shops which are striving to add a modern sense to sushi-making while maintaining and cherishing the traditional sushi-making methods, and may be said to be the representative way of today's sushi-making.

The art of sushi-making observed by sushi shops and explained in Chapters 1 and 2 differs somewhat from the way of sushi made at home in Chapter 3 "The Pleasure of Sushi-Making" with respect to materials and sushi-making methods, but these differences, if any, should be taken as variations. If the basic method of sushi-making is followed, to develop variations is yet another way of enjoying sushi-making.

## Special Terms Used in Sushi-Making

Sushi shops have their own technical terms and expressions. In this book, the writer has endeavored to use words and expressions easily understandable by ordinary people as much as possible. However, in order to help the reader have a peep into the real world of sushi, he has used some special terms and expressions which are italicized and are followed by their corresponding English words in parentheses. However, proper nouns and other untranslatable words are left as they are.

The word "sushi" has now acquired international acceptance, and therefore, was not italicized in this book. However, the "s" in sushi is voiced and "sushi" is pronounced "zushi" depending on the words that precede it. There is no difference at all between "sushi" and "zushi" as regards meaning.

In the same way, *tane* as ingredients for sushi is sometimes changed to *dane*. In this book, the word "sushi-*dane*" is used throughout instead of its English equivalent "sushi ingredients for *nigiri*-zushi".

## Calorie Count and Nutritional Information

As an aid to dieters, I have indicated the calorie count for each dish in Chater 3 "The Pleasure of Sushi-Making" along with the amounts of carbohydrates (excluding dietary fiber), protein, and fats and oils. The figures—or even when there are none—are all for servings per person. *The Japanese Food Composition Table* served as the basis for all of the calculations.

## Weights and Measures

The weights and measures used in the list of ingredients and cooking instructions for each recipe are given in both the metric and standard American-British system of pounds and ounces. British cooks measure many more items by weight than do Americans, who prefer cup measurements for items such as rice, flour, chopped vegetables, and so on. When following the recipes, use the measurement you are most comfortable with.

Liquid measurements present more of a problem when a book is to be used by cooks in different countries. The Japanese cup, for example, measures 200 ml, whereas the American cup is 236 ml, the British cup is 284 ml, and the Australian cup is 250 ml. We suggest you use the following conversion chart (tbs = tablespoons):

**Measures—Conversion Chart (Cup Measures)**

| Japanese Cup (In Book) | 1 cup | 2 cups | 3 cups | 4 cups |
|---|---|---|---|---|
| America adjusts to: | 1 cup −2 tbs | 1¾ cups −1 tbs | 2½ cups −1 tbs | 3½ cups −2 tbs |
| United Kingdom adjusts to: | ¾ cup −1 tbs | 1½ cups −2 tbs | 2 cups +2 tbs | 3¼ cups −1 tbs |
| Australia adjusts to: | ¾ cup +1 tbs | 1½ cups +2 tbs | 2½ cups −2 tbs | 3¼ cups −1 tbs |

## Tools and Ingredients

As for tools used for sushi-making, please refer to page 28, and as for ingredients, to corresponding items on pages 24–28.

You may use either Japanese or Californian rice. Californian rice is considered suitable when making sushi.

Use regular-type soy sauce. The light-type is not suitable for obtaining the maximum taste of sushi.

Use rice vinegar except under unavoidable circumstances. You had better use flavor-added rice vinegar (sushi-*zu*), which is available on the market.

As for rice wine, Japanese rice wine (*sake*) is considered to be the best.

# The World of Sushi

What is sushi? What is the origin of sushi? Who was the first to invent sushi? What is *Edomae*-zushi? What is the proper way of eating sushi? These and other similar questions cross one's mind when eating sushi, and it is just such types of questions that this book attempts to give an answer to.

# Varieties of Sushi—Tokyo Sushi

Sushi is represented in the world by *nigiri*-zushi (hand-formed sushi). However, there are numerous varieties of sushi in Japan.

In order to help you get a general idea of what sushi really is, we will show you what kinds of sushi exist in Tokyo (pages 10–11) and in the Kansai District (pages 14–15).

While *nigiri*-zushi is the most representative of the sushi originating in Tokyo, *Edo*-Style *Chirashi*-Zushi and *Tekka-Domburi* are also very popular with the Japanese people.

### *Nigiri*-Zushi (Hand-Formed Sushi)

This is the kind of sushi that are formed with the use of both hands. It has a relatively short history, and made its appearance in *Edo* (Tokyo) early in the 19th century. Fish and shellfish are the main sushi-*dane* for *nigiri*-zushi. The taste of *nigiri*-zushi depends more on the skill in forming it rather than on the quality of sushi-*dane*. *Maki*-zushi is also classed as *nigiri*-zushi.

## Edo-Style Chirashi-Zushi

Together with *nigiri*-zushi, this is a representative type stemming from Tokyo. In this style, various types of fish and shellfish are arranged on sushi rice.

## Tekka-Domburi

This is a kind of *Edo*-style *chirashi*-zushi. *Tekka* means red-hot iron, and at the same time, a slang word used for gamblers. In the world of sushi, however, it means red tuna meat put on sushi rice in an earthenware bowl. It is complete with thin sliced toasted seaweed spread on the tuna meat.

# The Birth and History of Sushi

## When and Where Sushi Was Born?

It is true that sushi is one of the representative foods of Japan today, but its origin is not found in Japan. When and where, then, did it come into existence? This is a very intriguing question.

The history of sushi is unexpectedly long. Sushi is mentioned for the first time in a dictionary compiled in China at the end of the 2nd century A.D. It was salted fish meat in rice, and was eaten after it was allowed to ferment. It is not clear whether the rice used was unpolished or polished as it is now. It appears that in those days only fish meat was eaten with the rice being discarded.

This sushi-making method is exactly like the way *funa*-zushi made in Shiga Prefecture in Japan. *Funa*-zushi, the oldest sushi left alive with a long history of more than 1,000 years, is said to be the starting point of sushi in Japan. Japanese records at the beginning of the 8th century A.D. before the birth of *funa*-zushi, mention something similar to sushi in which *awabi* (abalone) and *igai* (hard-shelled mussels) were used, but we can only conjecture about it, since no real factual knowledge is available.

So far as the history of sushi is concerned, it is certain that sushi made its debut earlier in China than in Japan. It is believed that sushi was introduced into Japan in about the 7th century A.D., though the exact date is not clear.

However, it would be too rash to conclude that sushi originated in China, for there is good reason to believe that sushi was introduced into China from a foreign country.

In countries other than Japan and China, there are foods closely resembling sushi, though they are not called by the name sushi. For instance, we have reports that foods prepared in much the same way as *funa*-zushi in Japan have been discovered in countries ranging from those at the foot of the Himalayas to Southeast Asian countries. I myself have recently visited North Borneo where I saw people, tribe of Iban, there making sushi-like food "kassam" prepared in their own way. I called sushi to mind instantly I ate this food.

Though we do not have evidence to state with positive certainty, many are of the opinion that it may have originated in some remote corners of Southeast Asia. Dr. Osamu Shinoda (1896–1978), an authority on Japanese sushi, writes in his *Book of Sushi* that sushi originated in Southeast Asia.

## Japanese Sushi and Sushi in Other Countries

It is interesting to find that many kinds of sushi have been developed in Japan but that in foreign countries sushi no longer exists or it exists in its original form at best. This fact is interesting if viewed in the light of sushi's relationship to rice.

Originally, sushi-making was a method of preserving fish by fermentation in those days when there were no refrigerators. In order to ferment fish, not only salt but also rice was needed. In China, sushi gradually came to be associated less with rice until rice was hardly used, and at the same time, sushi itself ceased to exist. In Southeast Asian countries, too, rice was used only to ferment fish.

By contrast, sushi came to be more and more closely related to rice in Japan until it developed into today's sushi which is eaten together with sushi rice.

Apart from the relationship between sushi and rice, we would like to emphasize here the decisive difference between Japanese and foreign sushi.

In Japan, sushi prepared in the same way as *funa*- zushi came to be called "*nare*-zushi", though it is not known from when. In making *nare*-zushi, a stone weight is always used in putting fish in salt and rice. But in other countries, the stone weight is not used, even if the fish and rice may be lightly pressed. In other words, the fish is just put in salt and rice.

The stone weight is of great significance. Whether the stone weight is heavy or light has a direct bearing not only on the taste of sushi but also on the length of time—it could be as long as three years—during which sushi can be preserved. Technically speaking, the stone weight serves to shut off air and to even the process of fermentation of lactic acid. In fact, the use of a stone weight or pressure is at the base of all the methods of preparing sushi in Japan.

## Three Types of Sushi in Japan

There are countless kinds of sushi in Japan if local varieties are included in the count. Sushi may be roughly classified into the three kinds of *nare*-zushi, *nama-nari*-zushi (also called "*nama-nare*") and *haya*-zushi.

As mentioned above, *nare*-zushi is an old, traditional sushi represented by *funa*-zushi. The fermentation period is said to have lasted from one to three years, and in principle, only the fish was eaten with the rice being discarded.

In the 15th century, *nama-nari*-zushi used the stone weight with a shorter fermentation time came into being. The fermentation time was about one month, and not only fish but also rice was eaten. In other words, *nama-nari*-zushi was eaten before the fish was not so well fermented as that of *nare*-zushi—or when the rice became sour to a certain extent and the fish was still raw, but its taste was beginning to become mellow as a result of the fermentation. *Kodai suzume*-zushi (see page 15) is said to have originally been a *nama-nari*-typed sushi. Even today, *nama-nari*-zushi using various kinds of fish and shellfish is made in Wakayama, Shiga and Gifu Prefectures (see page 94).

Be that as it may, *nama-nari*-zushi further deepened the connection between sushi and rice, and with its unique taste, it played an important role in advancing a step further the method of sushi-making.

This development was further spurred by the invention of the fermentation method using of vinegar. The use of vinegar made it possible to further shorten the fermentation time of sushi, which led to the development of *haya*-zushi in the middle of the 17th century. *Haya*-zushi was made by arranging in a wooden box, balls of sushi rice topped with slices of salted fish meat and by placing a stone weight on them just as a stone weight was used in making *nare*-zushi. This shortened the fermentation time to half a day or one night.

This was followed by other kinds of *haya*-zushi, *kiri*-zushi and *sasa-maki*-zushi. *Kiri*-zushi, which is said to be the origin of what we call *hako*-zushi today, was made in the following way. Sushi rice is put in a wooden box and sushi-*dane* are arranged on the rice. Then, a lid with a stone weight on it is placed on the sushi-*dane* and rice. Next, the rice with sushi-*dane* on it is cut into several pieces. *Sasa-maki*-zushi is the original form of what is called by the same name today. Cut pieces of sushi rice with *tane* on it are wrapped in bamboo leaves one by one and a stone weight is placed on them.

### *Nigiri*-Zushi Changed The History of Sushi

These varieties of sushi led to the development of various types of modern *haya*-zushi which are made without the use of any stone weights. Of special importance is the *nigiri*-zushi (hand-formed sushi) which made its debut in *Edo* (Tokyo) early in the 19th century. This completely changed the traditional image of sushi, and the most innovative part of it was that hands were used instead of a stone weight to make sushi. In other words, flexible pressure applied by both hands and their warmth played the role of the stone weight to a much better degree, and the fermentation period was made almost instantaneous.

Meanwhile, *nori-maki*-zushi (or *nori-maki* for short), which is also made with hands and the rolling bamboo mat without using the stone weight and is as popular as hand-formed sushi, came into

being toward the end of the 18th century, or earlier than hand-formed sushi.

*Hako*-zushi or box sushi, which is also called Osaka-zushi, originally used the stone weight, as explained above, but together with the popularity of hand-formed sushi, it came to be made by pressing a lid on it with both hands instead of using the stone weight. We owe this to the resourcefulness of sushi shops in Osaka.

*Saba*-zushi, which is a representative kind of sushi in Kyoto, appears to have been invented earlier than hand-formed sushi or during the transitional period from *nare*-zushi to *haya*-zushi. At first, it was prepared in the following way. The meat of mackerel salted and soaked in vinegar was sliced to a proper thickness, which is arranged on a kitchen cloth. Then, sushi rice formed in a rod-like shape was placed on them, and was wound with the slices of mackerel meat, and a weight was placed on it. Today, it is still wound in a kitchen cloth, but now is mostly pressed by the rolling bomboo mat and hands without a weight. It tastes better if it is eaten after a certain time during which it "matures".

The more controversial of the other kinds of sushi is *chirashi*-zushi, which is called *bara*-zushi in the Kansai District. Neither a weight nor hands are used to make it. However, originally, this sushi, too, was made by pressing sushi rice, mixed with various kinds of "*gu*" (ingredients), in a wooden box with a weight.

*Tekka-maki* and *Tekka-domburi* were new kinds of sushi which made their appearance at the beginning of the 19th century. *Tekka-maki* is *nori-maki* with cut tuna meat as the core, while *tekka-domburi*, which was called "*azuma-domburi*" (*Azuma* means Tokyo and its neighboring areas) until the beginning of the 20th century, is so to speak, *chirashi*-zushi with sliced tuna meat on it.

There are many other kinds of sushi in Japan, of which the more important are illustrated on page 94. Furthermore, *bara*-zushi in Okayama Prefecture and *sake*-zushi in Kagoshima Prefecture, which are shown in the following photos have a long history, and are peculiar to these districts.

Bara-Zushi         Sake-Zushi

# Varieties of Sushi——Sushi in The Kansai District

Sushi in the Kansai District, including Osaka and Kyoto, have a longer history than Tokyo sushi. Particularly, the *hako*-zushi (box-sushi) of Osaka and the *saba*-zushi of Kyoto are as popular as *nigiri*-zushi.

### Kansai-Style *Bara*-Zushi

This is a kind of *chirashi*-zushi with egg roll cut into thin thread-like pieces, shrimp, sea bream, *anago* and other *tane* placed on sushi rice. It differs from *Edo*- style *chirashi*-zushi in that the kinds of *tane* used are much fewer in number, with special emphasis being given to the taste of rice, as these types of *tane* are mixed with rice.

### *Mushi*-Zushi (Steamed Sushi)

A unique sushi originating from the Kansai District in the latter half of the 19th century. Kansai-style *chirashi*-zushi is served after being steamed. It is a kind of sushi suitable for cold winter days.

### *Hako*-Zushi (Box Sushi)

*Hako*-zushi is also called Osaka-zushi, and is a representative sushi of Osaka. Its history is older than that of *nigiri*-zushi. Sushi-*dane* and sushi rice are put in a box-like frame and are pressed from above.

### *Saba*-Zushi (Mackerel Sushi)

A kind of sushi from the Kansai District designed to bring out the unique taste of mackerel. The most representative type of this is the *saba*-zushi of Kyoto, which is called the *bō*-zushi of mackerel.

### *Kodai-Suzume*-Zushi
### (Sparrow Sushi of Young Sea Bream)

This sushi has a long history, and is said to have existed as far back as the 17th century. Originally, it was shaped like a sparrow, deriving its name from the shape. Though it is called *kodai* (young sea bream)-zushi, the *tane* was originally not young sea bream but young gray mullet.

# Origin and Development of *Nigiri*-Zushi

As explained in the preceding section "The Birth and History of Sushi", of various kinds of sushi, *nigiri*-zushi (hand-formed sushi) has a relatively short history of 160 to 170 years at most.

However, there is no doubt that *nigiri*-zushi was developed as food for the common people, but there are many doubtful points regarding exactly where and how *nigiri*-zushi first came into existence. Moreover, *nigiri*-zushi has undergone a lot of changes together with the passage of time.

## Theories About The Origin of *Nigiri*-Zushi

There are more than a few theories about the origin of *nigiri*-zushi. According to one theory, they were invented by Yohei Hanaya (1799–1858), the first proprietor of Yohei-Zushi Shop at Ryogoku in *Edo* or Tokyo of today. This is the best-known story about the origins of *nigiri*-zushi.

However, it is very difficult to accept this story as it is. Yohei-Zushi Shop was in business until about 1930, and there is no doubt that it was one of the oldest shops of *nigiri*-zushi. But there are historical records which say that there were some people who invented *nigiri*-zushi well before Yohei. Therefore, it seems to be more correct to say that he was a successful developer of *nigiri*-zushi rather than an inventor.

## Why *Nigiri*-Zushi Is Called *Edomae*-Zushi?

It was after World War II that *nigiri*-zushi became popular throughout Japan. At the same time, the word *Edomae*-zushi came to be used for *nigiri*-zushi, and is still used as such today.

What does the word *Edomae* mean? Originally, it meant the sea in front of the *Edo* Castle, and at the same time, fish and shellfish caught in that sea. To make a more detailed explanation, there was the Bay of Tokyo just in front of the *Edo* Castle, which is today's Imperial Palace, a sea which once abounded in high quality fish and shellfish. In the early 17th century, *Edomae* meant a certain area in the Bay of Tokyo, or as it were, a fishing ground.

Consequently, *Edomae*-zushi meant not only *nigiri*-zushi using fish or shellfish caught in a certain area of the Bay of Tokyo but also sushi using high quality fish or shellfish.

However, today the Bay of Tokyo has been reclaimed to a sizable extent and has been unrecognizably changed from what it was in the *Edo* period (17th–19th C.), and the high quality fish of that period can no more be found in the waters of the Bay of Tokyo. Naturally enough, sushi shops can no longer depend on the Bay of Tokyo for a good selection of fish and shellfish, but have to depend on all the seas of the world, let alone the seas of Japan, for the supply of fish and shellfish they use.

There were shops which used the word *Edomae* before sushi shops. More than 200 years ago, shops which served cooked eels caught in the *Edomae* rivers or rivers in front of the *Edo* Castle, used the word *Edomae* as their catchphrase. But they ceased to use the word about 100 years ago when *Edomae* eels ceased to be caught there.

The word was revived by sushi shops after World War II, and finally meant all kinds of *nigiri*-zushi. The word *Edomae* sounds empty to me and would to many others if one thinks of the original meaning of the word *Edomae* and the present state of sushi-*dane* served by sushi shops.

## There Were Two Types of Sushi Shops

At present, most sushi shops have a counter and tables, where customers are served, and at the same time, they deliver sushi to customers, and sell sushi which customers take home as "souvenirs". This is not the way sushi shops operated formerly, but a style of business which became prevalent after World War II.

At least until the beginning of this century, sushi shops were classed into two types, ordinary indoor shops (*uchi-mise*) and outdoor sushi stands (*yatai*). Some *uchi-mise*-type sushi shops had small matted rooms where customers were able to eat sushi. However, most sushi shops made sushi for delivery to customers or for sushi customers to take home. In contrast, *yatai* or sushi stands served customers on the spot. At first, they were mostly knockdown-type stands, but were later made movable by affixing wheels to them. Customers did not sit on chairs but ate sushi, buffet style. However, as *yatai* became popular, more and more *uchi-mise* provided stands at their entrance.

*Yatai* in the old days

Those who wanted to eat sushi the light, carefree way, went to sushi stands. In those days, sushi was relatively low in price, and eating sushi was one of the pleasures of the common people. It is a matter for great regret that today sushi has become high-priced food and is served at high-class shops, in which the common people enter only occasionally.

## Arrange Sushi As If to Draw A Landscape

On pages 18 and 19 you will see color photos showing how sushi should be arranged to be served. These pictures also show that the arrangement of sushi has changed along with time.

Arranging sushi may seem to be easy, but it is unexpectedly difficult. This technique is acquired in the last stage of learning the art of sushi-making. This is because arranging sushi is the same as drawing a beautiful landscape in the sushi container. Sushi makers of old arranged sushi in the spirit of a painter, and actually sushi-makers were told by their seniors to get hints from the noted paintings of the time.

Today, *nigiri*-zushi are arranged in several different styles, but all these styles are intended to emphasize the color effect. Usually, they are arranged on a bit of an angle one by one to give full play to the color and beauty.

In prewar days, however, sushi were not arranged on a flat surface, but were piled one upon another in layers. They used to say "pile sushi one upon another" instead of saying "arrange sushi side by side".

Sushi were piled one upon another in different ways at different shops. I myself once served sushi in the four-piled style and the six-piled style. In the four-piled style, three sushi were arranged below with one on top, and in the six-piled style, four sushi were placed below with two on top. Cut bamboo leaves were inserted between the lower and upper layer.

Before my time, sushi were piled one upon another in five or six layers, or in a pyramid style, *tane* by *tane*, and my parents who are no longer with me, used to tell me how beautiful sushi piled in the pyramid style looked.

In prewar days, sushi shops hated to arrange sushi on a flat surface as is common today. If one delivered sushi arranged in a flat style to an ordinary home, they would get angry and say, "We are respectable people. Do not deliver *daiya* sushi to us." *Daiya* were shops serving Japanese dishes, including sushi, which specially catered to those enjoying themselves in the licensed quarters (entertainment area) in the past. *Daiya* shops arranged sushi in the flat way. They arranged sushi on a flat surface so as to give the impression that there were a lot of sushi. They also used a lot of bamboo leaves, so much so that such sushi were called "tiger-lurking sushi". In Japanese and Chinese paintings, tigers were usually painted in a forest of bamboo.

However, the present way of arranging sushi in the flat style definitely has its advantages. For instance, sushi with *nikiri* (see page 28) or *nitsume* (see page 65) sauce on them can remain clean, with the shape of the sushi continuing to be maintained. Furthermore, it does not take a great deal of time to arrange sushi in this way.

Though the licensed quarters were abolished after the war and *daiya* shops have ceased to exist, it is interesting to note that a style once despised, has become the most popular way of serving sushi.

## Sizes and Shapes of *Nigiri*-Zushi

Sushi is smaller in size today than they were about 50 years ago. Formerly, the standard size of *nigiri*-zushi was "*hitokuchi-han*" or a bite and a half, not only at *uchi-mise* but also at *yatai*.

In those days, if a sushi maker delivered small-sized *nigiri*-zushi without a special order for them, the customer might have said spitefully, "What are these? You ought not to have delivered small-sized sushi like these to a respectable home like ours. What happened! Did you run out of rice?" Unless specially ordered, small-sized sushi was looked down on not only by respectable homes but also even in licensed quarters.

It must be added here, however, that what is important is not the size but the balance between the amount of *tane* and that of sushi rice.

I would like to mention here that sushi is formed differently according to different sushi makers. However, the following four shapes are the most representative ones. Of which side view profiles can be seen illustrated below. The *tawara* shape sushi resembles a straw bag in which unhulled rice was contained formerly, while the *jigami* shape sushi looks like a piece of paper pasted on a fan. The *kushi* shape sushi is shaped like a Japanese-style comb which women use to comb their long hair with, and the *funa-zoko* sushi resembles the shape of a ship.

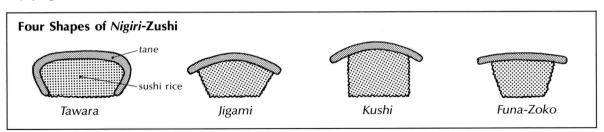

## Four Shapes of *Nigiri*-Zushi

tane

sushi rice

Tawara          Jigami          Kushi          Funa-Zoko

# Artistic Arrangement of *Nigiri*-Zushi

*Nigiri*-Zushi for one person or several persons are arranged to be served, or are put in a box to be taken home. The arrangement of *nigiri*-zushi may appear simple, but actually it is rather difficult. The point is to arrange them in the same way a painter would draw a beautiful landscape. So, a good sushi maker is required to have something of a painter in him.

**Nagashi-Mori** (*Nagashi* meaning arrangement)
This is the most common way of arranging sushi. Each sushi is arranged on a slight angle. The photo shows an arrangement of *nigiri*-zushi for four to five persons.

**Hōsha-Mori** (Radial Arrangement)
A modern arrangement style. This type is placed in a circular pattern so that the sushi in a sense is always facing the customers. The photo shows an arrangement of sushi for three to four persons.

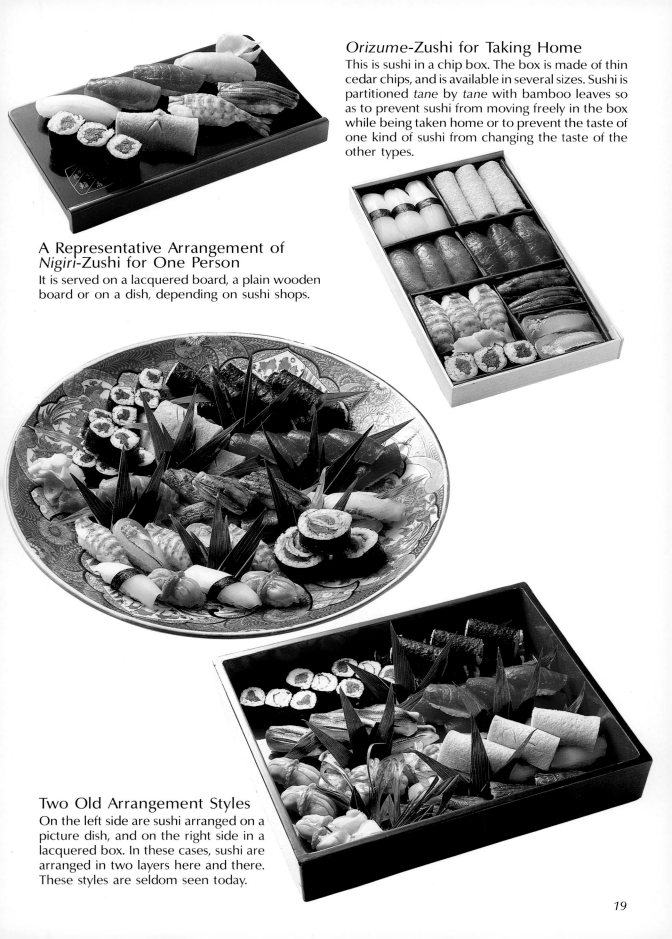

## Orizume-Zushi for Taking Home
This is sushi in a chip box. The box is made of thin cedar chips, and is available in several sizes. Sushi is partitioned *tane* by *tane* with bamboo leaves so as to prevent sushi from moving freely in the box while being taken home or to prevent the taste of one kind of sushi from changing the taste of the other types.

## A Representative Arrangement of *Nigiri*-Zushi for One Person
It is served on a lacquered board, a plain wooden board or on a dish, depending on sushi shops.

## Two Old Arrangement Styles
On the left side are sushi arranged on a picture dish, and on the right side in a lacquered box. In these cases, sushi are arranged in two layers here and there. These styles are seldom seen today.

# Proper Way of Eating *Nigiri*-Zushi

Since sushi has developed as food for the common people, there are no established formalities for eating sushi.

However, actually, there are some common rules that are taken for granted by sushi eaters, sushi shops and sushi journalists. It would be all right if these were well founded and reasonable, but the trouble is that many of them are erroneously based. I think it is about time that these types of old-fashioned rules should be done away with.

## Some Sushi Are Well Formed, Others Are Not

You will feel embarrassed if sushi-*dane* should slip off from a piece of sushi or sushi rice should fall apart while being eaten. This is not the fault of the person eating the sushi, the blame should go to the sushi maker who formed it.

*Nigiri*-Zushi is not just a ball of rice topped with a piece of sushi-*dane*. Good *nigiri*-zushi requires sushi-*dane* to be securely stuck to sushi rice.

Formerly, sushi makers used to say that sushi-making was an art that it took their whole lifetime to accomplish.

Though seemingly simple, sushi-making is difficult and delicate work.

## *Nigiri*-Zushi Should Not Be Fishy

You cannot eat good-tasting sushi if it smells fishy when you put it into your mouth. Use of fish meat not fresh enough and having a bad smell is definitely out of the question.

Fish and shellfish used as sushi-*dane* are eaten raw in many cases, so that it is only natural that they be of the freshest quality. You may think that it is only natural for a certain amount of the fishy smell to exist. However, this way of thinking is actually false.

At least, sushi makers in the prewar period were ashamed of serving *nigiri*-zushi which had a fishy smell. In those days, refrigeration was at a very low level and there was not a plentiful supply of water as exists today. Therefore, they paid the utmost attention to all processes of sushi-making, including the preparation of sushi-*dane* and the handling of kitchen knives so as to prevent their customers from suffering from food-poisoning. It was there that they could give full play to their sushi-making skill.

If a sushi maker serves fishy *nigiri*-zushi today when he has sufficient refrigeration at his disposal and can use as much water as he wants, we must say that he is not yet skilled enough in the art of sushi-making.

At the sushi shop *"Yoshino-Zushi-Honten"*

## Is There Some Order in Eating *Nigiri*-Zushi?

Let's take an imaginary customer sitting at the counter of a sushi shop ordering *nigiri*-zushi. You must have heard people say that you should begin with *tamago-yaki* ( sushi omelet which sushi makers call "*gyoku*").

It is true that this was a reasonable saying during the prewar period. Formerly, sushi shops made their own omelet as *tane* for their *nigiri*-zushi. The seasoning and baking of an omelet is the most complex work of all preparations for sushi-*dane*. Therefore, it was said that if you ate *tamago-yaki* first, you could quickly evaluate the skill of the sushi maker. Eating *tamago-yaki* was, so to speak, a test of the skill of the sushi maker.

But in recent years, the majority of sushi shops in Japan purchase ready-made omelet on the market, so that we cannot attach much meaning to this saying anymore. I was told by a senior authority on sushi, "Mr. Yoshino, most are of the opinion that *gyoku* should be eaten first when enjoying sushi. However, my question to them is, What if *gyoku* tasted badly? Wouldn't you be a bit outdated, if you seriously stuck to this useless rule. I would even dare to say that *gyoku* is more like a kind of dessert for Western dishes. In other words, it should rightfully be eaten last."

I would like to say definitely here that there is no order at all in eating *nigiri*-zushi according to different sushi-*dane*. You have only to eat the kind of *nigiri*-zushi that strikes your fancy.

## Should *Nigiri*-Zushi Be Eaten with One's Fingers or with Chopsticks?

A word is in order about how to eat *nigiri*-zushi for there are different opinions about this.

There are many sushi shops which do not provide chopsticks to customers sitting at the counter, as if to say that *nigiri*-zushi should be eaten with one's fingers. If a customer asks a sushi maker to provide him with chopsticks, there are surprising cases in which the sushi maker looks as if to say that the customer does not know how to eat *nigiri-zushi*.

Originally, both sushi makers of indoor shops (*uchi-mise*) and those of outdoor stands (*yatai*) formed sushi while sitting. If customers wanted to eat good-tasting *nigiri*-zushi, they preferred eating at these types of stands. In this case, they stood in front of the sitting sushi maker as he went about his business of making sushi. As they were standing, the most comfortable and natural way for them to eat sushi was by using their fingers.

But the situation has done a complete turn today. The sushi maker now stands, while the customers sit on chairs. Due to this position, some customers find it difficult to eat sushi well using their fingers. In such a case and particularly for certain types, chopsticks are the most natural way to enjoy sushi. In the case of women, it would be all right for them to take sushi on a small dish first and eat them from the dish with chopsticks, a more lady-like approach to eating sushi.

Whatever the case, there are no set rules at all which require customers to eat *nigiri*-zushi using their fingers. Chopsticks may be used if one feels more comfortable eating in this way. For your information, here is an illustration showing the one way to hold and handle chopsticks.

### Are There Any Rules for Picking Up Sushi with Your Fingers?

Let me give my opinion first. There is no set rule in regard to this. You have only to eat sushi in the most natural, easy-to-eat way.

But the trouble is that there is what they call a "correct way of eating sushi." You may have heard of it once or twice.

According to this "correct way of eating," you should hold sushi as if to cover the top part, raising the other side. Naturally, in this case, the *tane* faces downward. Then, you should dip the sushi lightly in soy sauce, and turning the other end toward

## Sasa-Giri (Cut Bamboo Leaves)

Cut bamboo leaves are used to make sushi look beautiful when they are arranged. At the same time, they are used as a sort of fence to prevent some kinds of sushi (for instance, *nitsume*-applied *nimono-dane*) from coming into direct contact with each other. They are cut into many different shapes to please the eye.

you, and put it into your mouth.

Even established sushi shops formally declare this to be the "correct" way to eat sushi. However, there are some sushi-*dane*, that you would find great difficulty eating in this way. If the *tane* does not adhere well to sushi rice, it could fall off. This so-called "correct" way has its origin dating back about a hundred years ago, when a certain politician used this style for fun when eating sushi at a certain party. Therefore, the "correctness" of this way of eating is entirely groundless.

It would be far easier if you place sushi sideways and pick it up lightly with the thumb and forefinger, or with the thumb and middle finger, placing the forefinger on the *tane*.

In my opinion, the most important thing is that sushi be enjoyed, how you handle it is secondary. There is one thing, however, which I have to call your attention to. Sometimes we see people taking *tane* off from sushi rice and put it again on sushi rice after dipping it in soy sauce. You may do this in eating *chirashi*-zushi, but when it comes to *nigiri*-zushi, this is not only viewed with great disappointment by the sushi maker, but also the worst way to eat *nigiri*-zushi.

### How to Use Chopsticks

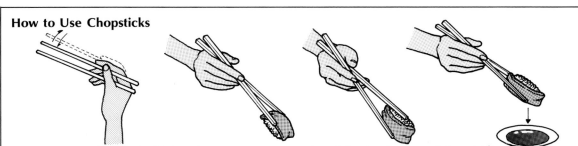

Chopsticks are handled with four fingers excepting the small finger. A pair of chopsticks are held between the thumb and the forefinger, and the lower chopstick is held by the third finger at around its second joint, while the upper chopstick held by the tips of the forefinger and the middle finger. When picking up some thing with chopsticks, move the upper chopstick while holding the lower chopstick in a fixed position. An example of how to hold sushi with chopsticks is illustrated here.

# Basic Technique of Making Sushi

## How to Make Sushi Rice

Sushi rice is one of the main factors determining the taste of sushi. Formerly, it was believed that Japanese short-grained rice was the only rice that was suitable for sushi-making. However, Californian rice is equally as good.

The method of cooking rice to be used for sushi is entirely different from the Western-style cooking. Today, it is easy to cook rice if you use an electric or gas rice cooker. However, if you do not have such a rice cooker, you had better use an aluminum pot with a heavy lid. In the latter case, cook rice in the following way. (In the case of using gas as the heat source).

**1.** Wash rice for 30 minutes before cooking in summer and for 1 hour before in winter. Wash it well changing the water several times until the water becomes as clear as pure water. Then put rice into a bamboo basket.

**2.** Put rice in a pot together with about the same amount of water as rice or 10 percent more water than that. Put a lid on the pot and boil it under high heat.

**3.** Reduce to medium heat about 1 minute after the water begins to boil, and when the surface of rice becomes visible, reduce to low heat. Then, when there is no water in the pot, switch the heat to high heat and leave it for about 10 seconds, and then turn off the heat.

**4.** Leave rice in the pot for 14 to 15 minutes to allow it to steam.

### How to Mix Vinegar with Seasonings

Vinegar is mixed with seasonings in different ways at different sushi shops. However, originally only vinegar and salt were used to season sushi rice. Today, many sushi shops add sugar as well. At my shop, I use the following mixing ratio.

> 16¼ cups of rice
> 1¼ cups of vinegar (red vinegar)
> 2½ ounces (60 g) of unrefined salt

In other words, the mixing ratio is 1 tablespoon of vinegar and 1 teaspoon of unrefined salt for one cup of rice.

Move boiled and steamed rice to a *hankiri* (wooden vessel) which has been wiped well with a wet dishcloth.

Sprinkle hot rice evenly with vinegar prepared as explained above through a bag filter.

Spread rice by raising rice from the bottom with a wooden ladle.

Mix rice using a wooden ladle as if cutting through the rice so that vinegar may spread through rice. Never mix rice in such a way as to knead it.

When vinegar has been spread all over, cool rice with a fan. An electric fan may be used instead of a fan. Never fan it while mixing vinegar with rice.

Turn rice with the wooden ladle so that rice at the bottom may be cooled.

## How to Form Sushi

However good sushi-*dane* and sushi rice may be, no *nigiri*-zushi tastes well, if it is not formed well. Each sushi maker forms sushi in a slightly different way, but the point is to form sushi in such a way that sushi-*dane* may stick to sushi rice well. If sushi-*dane* falls off from sushi or if sushi rice falls apart, such *nigiri*-zushi cannot be called sushi.

## How to Form Sushi

Pick a piece of sushi-*dane* up with the thumb and the forefinger of the left hand. Do not put it in the palm of your hand so that sushi-*dane* may not be warmed even a little by body temperature.

Take with the right hand an amount of sushi rice proper for the size of the sushi-*dane* you have selected, and form sushi rice in a rod- or cylinder-like shape.

With sushi rice in the right hand, scoop up some *wasabi* with the tip of the forefinger of the right hand, and put it in the center of *tane*.

Place sushi rice on *tane*, and put the thumb of the left hand at the end of sushi rice. Press sushi rice with the two fingers with a proper amount of pressure. This pressure is the most important point.

It is important that *tane* sticks closely to sushi rice in the preceding stage (4). Then, turn the right hand, and place the left hand on it as if to cover it with the left hand.

Move sushi to the left hand, and again press it with the forefinger and middle finger of the right hand. Repeat the processes described in (4) to (6) once or twice.

Turn sushi in the palm of your left hand so that *tane* faces upward. A skilled sushi maker can do this using only his left hand. However, you may use your right hand as well to do this.

Hold sushi at one end of it with the thumb of the left hand, and use the remaining four fingers and the forefinger and the middle finger of the right hand to press sushi.

# How to Make *Nori-Maki*-Zushi (Sushi Rolls)

*Nori-maki*-zushi is as important to sushi shops as *nigiri*-zushi. If they are not wrapped in the proper way, they will differ in size, sushi rice will come out or *nori* (toasted seaweed) will break up into pieces. The point is to pay attention to the amount of sushi rice and also to the force of the tips of the fingers of both hands with which sushi rice is pressed. It is also important to wrap sushi rice as quickly as possible.

**In the case of thin sushi rolls**

Place a *nori* sheet cut in half on the rolling bamboo mat, with one end of *nori* at the front end of the rolling mat. Form sushi rice in a rod-like shape, spreading it from left to right on *nori*.

Spread sushi rice evenly, but leave some space at the top and bottom of *nori*, and make a groove for the "*gu*" sideways in the center by pressing sushi rice with the thumbs of both hands.

Put in the groove two or three lengths of seasoned gourd strips as long as the width of *nori*.

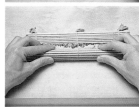

Lift sushi rice together with the rolling mat from the front side, and push the mat to the end of the other side of sushi rice. Then, draw the mat to the front and press it with both hands.

Roll the rolling mat lightly from the front to the other side, wrap sushi rice with it and press sushi rice again with both hands.

Remove the rolling mat and shape *maki-zushi* well by pressing it from both ends.

# Changes in Ingredients for *Nigiri*-Zushi

## Tuna Changed *Nigiri*-Zushi

*Tane* has changed very much since *nigiri*-zushi (hand-formed sushi) first made its appearance. Particularly, the discovery of *maguro* (tuna) as sushi-*dane* rapidly developed hand-formed sushi. At the same time, tuna was able to give full play to its real value thanks to hand-formed sushi.

It was about the middle of 19th century that tuna came to be used as sushi-*dane*. In those days, tuna was regarded as a low-cost fish. Therefore, high-class sushi shops refrained from using tuna.

It was probably outdoor sushi stands that first used tuna as sushi-*dane*. They used only red-meat tuna, which they kept dipped in soy sauce. It is because of this that even today some people call red-meat tuna "*zuke*" (dipped meat). *Toro* (oily part of tuna meat), which is popular today as a high-class sushi-*dane*, was regarded as the lowest of the low-class *tane*. In other words, it was completely ignored. I would like to bring to your attention that it was about in 1918 that the name "*toro*" first came to be used, and to tell the truth, the person who so named it, was a customer of my father who was the owner of our shop at the time. It was named *toro* (melt) for it feels as if the *tane* melts in your mouth.

Not only tuna meat was dipped in soy sauce before use, but in former days, even white-meat fish was soaked not in soy sauce but in vinegar. White-meat fish were lightly salted and were dipped in sweetened vinegar or plain vinegar.

Even shellfish was not used in its raw form. In most cases, it was passed through boiling water and was dipped in sweetened vinegar. This was true for all clams with the exception of *akagai* (red clam) which was eaten raw after being quickly dipped in vinegar. Clams were cooked in the same way in the past as they are today. They were served after being boiled once and dipped in boiled lightly sweetened soy sauce.

Cuttlefish and squid were boiled and were either dipped in sweetened vinegar (*su-ika*) or cooked with soy sauce with sugar (*ni-ika*). It was in the postwar period that they came to be eaten raw.

As for octopus, raw octopus was eaten after being quickly boiled in soy sauce with sugar. Sushi shops which used boiled octopus were regarded as third-rate shops. Furthermore, as for shellfish, *aoyagi* (skimmer) was not used by first-class shops. This sushi-*dane* also became popular during the postwar period.

Among the sushi-*dane* that are not used so much today is *shira-uo* (whitebait). It was once

very popular from December through February when it was caught in the Bay of Tokyo. If it is used in any of the shops today, it is served raw in almost all cases. Formerly, it was boiled with a small amount of salt and sugar carefully so that the shape of the fish might be maintained, and four to five of them were placed on a piece of sushi, and tied boiled gourd strips or thin strips of *nori* (toasted seaweed).

## In Former Days, Sushi-*Dane* Were Seasonal

It was in the postwar period that sushi-*dane* came to be eaten raw with new types of sushi-*dane* making their appearance.

However, the big change that occurred at this time was that sushi-*dane* ceased to be strongly associated with different seasons. Japan has four distinct seasons, and Japanese dishes are characterized by the use of seasonal materials. This was also true with sushi.

For instance, in autumn *shinko* (young *kohada*= young gizzard shad) was offered, and when the spring breezes began to blow, such shining *tane* as *kisu* (sillago) and *sayori* (halfbeak) were highly sought after. In May, clams and red clams were no longer offered, nor were they available on the market. In summer, the shellfish that was offered was steamed abalone seasoned either with salt or rice wine and the only shining *tane* was horse mackerel. If a customer ordered *kohada* in summer, the sushi shop proprietor would have probably said sharply, "*Kohada*? It is now swimming in the waters off Hawaii. You cannot find any in Japanese waters."

Now that none of the numerous types of sushi-*dane* that used to be plentiful in the Bay of Tokyo can be found, sushi shops have to depend for the most part on imported fish and shellfish. It is no wonder that sushi-*dane* are available throughout the year, and have ceased to be associated with seasons. Nevertheless, it would be better to eat sushi-*dane* in their respective seasons.

## A Sense of Color in Hand-Formed Sushi

The thing that has remained unchanged about sushi is that sushi is associated with different colors. Recently, an American sushi enthusiast asked me, "You say 'red, white, and blue,' what do these colors signify?"

Needless to say, these words mean the kinds of sushi-*dane*, and sushi makers and eaters began using these words in the 1920s.

"Red" means red-meat fish, including tuna and similar fish, as well as bonito. "White" means white-meat fish, specifically flounder in former days. Today, it includes *tai* (sea bream), *suzuki* (sea bass), *karei* (halibut), *hiramasa* (amber jack), *shima-aji* (yellow jack), *kanpachi, me-dai,* and *ishi-dai.* Those that are referred to as "blue" are the so-called *"hikari-mono"* (shining *tane* fish), such as *kohada, sayori, aji* (horse mackerel), *saba* (mackerel) and *kisu*. Both red-meat and white-meat fish are called "raw" *tane* fish, which are eaten raw, while shining *tane* fish are sprayed lightly with salt and are soaked in vinegar.

When I gave the above explanation, the American thanked me saying, "Though the colors are few, these colors not only show the kinds of *tane* but also suggest their tastes. I think I can enjoy eating sushi even more with this bit of knowledge."

The other sushi-*dane* are "nimono", which include *anago* (conger eel), *hamaguri* (clam), *tako* (octopus), *ika* (squid), and *shako* (mantis shrimp), which are used after being boiled or cooked with soy sauce with sugar. Squid, however, is classed as raw *tane* when it is served raw.

Shellfish *tane* are represented by *aka-gai* (red clam), *awabi* (abalone), *tori-gai* (cockle), *mirugai* (horse-neck clam), *hotate-gai* (scallop), *aoyagi* (skimmer), *kobashira* (adductor of skimmer), etc.

As for boiled shrimp and omelet, they have been classified differently. Here, let me classify them as "nimono" according to my own opinion. However, raw shrimp (called "odori") should be classed as a raw *tane*.

## Side Ingredients Are Essential to Sushi

Fish and shellfish play a principal role in sushi-making, but side materials which include dried vegetables, vegetables, spices, and seasonings are also important to bring out the various tastes of sushi.

### Dried Vegetables and Seaweed

They include *kampyo* (seasoned gourd strips), *shii-take* (mushroom), *nori* (toasted seaweed) and *konbu* (kelp).

*Kampyo* is dried long and narrow strips of the fruit meat of a plant similar to a calabash, and is an essential material for *nori-maki* (sushi rolls) and *chirashi*-zushi (mixed sushi). Some sushi shops use raw *shiitake* after roasting it. However, dried *shiitake* is used for *nori-maki* and *chirashi*-zushi in almost all cases. Dried *shiitake* has a unique, pleasant smell which is lacking in raw *shiitake*.

*Nori* (toasted seaweed) is made by drying thinly spread *nori* and looks like a sheet of paper. In the Kanto District around Tokyo, *nori* is roasted before use, but in the Kansai District around Osaka and Kyoto, dried *nori* is used as it is. Depending on uses, a whole sheet of *nori* is used, or it is cut into half. In other cases, it is cut into thin strips or torn into small pieces.

*Konbu* (kelp) is also a kind of seaweed, and is in its dried form when it reaches the market. It is used mainly in the making of broths.

### Vegetables and Spices

A representative vegetable used as sushi-*dane* is the cucumber, which is used as the base ingredient for *nori-maki*. Japanese cucumbers are smaller and thinner than European and American ones, and as the seeds are soft, they can be eaten together with the seeds. It appears that cucumbers began to be used as the core of *nori-maki* in the latter half of the 1920s, but the exact date is not known.

*Kaiware-na* (sprouts of long white radish) and *mitsuba* (trefoil) have come to be used as sushi-*dane* only recently.

*Negi, wakegi* (kinds of Welsh onions) and *asatsuki* (chives) began to be used recently to add more flavor to sushi and bring out the taste. These can be compared to lemon used with Western dishes.

The more important are ginger and *wasabi* (Japanese horseradish), which are as important today as they were in the past. Of all of them, the most commonly used is raw ginger. It is grated and used as a savoring for sushi, or is cut into thin slices, which are fermented in vinegar. These slices are eaten to kill the aftertaste of sushi.

*Wasabi* is used either raw or in its powdered form. Powdered *wasabi* mainly consists of horseradish. Sushi shops, journalists and sushi eaters say that only those shops that use raw radish can be called first-class sushi shops. However, I do not think so. At a time when the production of *wasabi* is limited and its price is so high as it is today, many sushi shops will become high-class shops or go bankrupt if they stick to using raw *wasabi*. As powdered *wasabi* has now been improved in quality and has its own distinct flavor, it would be necessary to recognize its claim to existence, a claim distinct from that of raw *wasabi*. (The price of raw *wasabi* is several times higher than that of powdered *wasabi*).

### Seasonings

Vinegar, soy sauce, *sake* (rice wine), *mirin* (sweet rice wine for cooking), salt and sugar are the main seasonings, of which the most important are vinegar and soy sauce.

Vinegar is decisive in that whether you can make goodtasting sushi or not depends on its use. Therefore, it is necessary to examine the quality of vinegar. Three kinds of vinegar are used for sushi-making. The first is made from rice, and the second from *sake* lees and the third from fruit. My own shop uses vinegar selected from among various kinds of vinegar made from *sake* lees.

Soy sauce is used in many ways. It is used as

(continued on page 28)

# Ingredients for *Nigiri*-Zushi

Fish and shellfish are the main sushi-*dane*. But vegetables are also important. Furthermore, dried foods, spices and seasonings play minor roles in the making of *Nigiri*-Zushi.

## Fish and Shellfish

There are more than 30 kinds of fish and shellfish that are used as sushi-*dane*. Other than those which are shown in the photos are *suzuki* (sea bass), *hamachi* (young yellowtail), *anago* (conger eel), octopus, sea urchin, and fish roe.

From front left,
*Kuruma-Ebi* (Wheel Shrimp)
*Bakagai (Aoyagi)* (Skimmer)
*Akagai* (Red Clam)
*Mirugai* (Horse-Neck Clam)
*Awabi* (Abalone)
*Yari-Ika* (Squid)
*Surume-Ika* (Squid)
*Meji-Maguro* (Young Tuna)
*Hirame* (Flounder)
*Kisu* (Sillago)
*Kohada* (Gizzard Shad)
*Ama-Ebi* (Sweet Shrimp)
*Aji* (Horse Mackerel)
*Hotategai* (Scallop)
*Kasugo* (Young Sea Bream)
*Saba* (Mackerel)
*Sayori* (Halfbeak)
*Hamaguri* (Clam)
*Shima-Aji* (Yellow Jack)
*Tairagai* (Tairagi Shellfish)

## Vegetables

Vegetables used for sushi are limited. Vegetables are essential for sushi as main sushi-*dane* or as a sort of setoff for sushi.

From front, *Kaiware-na* (Sprouts of White Radish), *Mitsuba* (Honewort), *Asatsuki* (Chives), and *Negi* (Welsh Onion)

From left, *Morokyu* (Small Cucumber), Cucumber

## Dried Foods

Some dried foods are used as sushi-*dane*, materials for *maki-zushi* (sushi rolls), or as materials for stock.

From front, Dried *Shiitake* (Mushrooms), *Kampyo* (Dried Gourd Strips), *Konbu* (Kelp), *Nori* (Toasted Seaweed).

## Flavorings and Spices

These are used as a setoff for sushi or to kill the aftertaste of sushi.

From front left, *Aojiso* (Beefsteak Plant), *Myogatake*, *Hanahojiso*, (center) Lemon;
From top left, *Bofu*, *Daikon* (Radish), *Ogo-nori* (a kind of Seaweed)

Raw *Wasabi* (Japanese Green Horseradish)

Powdered *Wasabi*

Ginger, Ginger Soaked in Vinegar

# Seasonings

Soy Sauce: from left, Regular-type 150 ml, 250 ml, Milder-type 500 ml, 250 ml

*Mirin* (*Hon-Mirin*) (Sweet Rice Wine for Cooking)

Vinegar: left, brewed (*Yone-zu*); right, flavor-added (*Sushi-Zu*)

Left, *Katsuo-Dashi* (Extract of Bonito), right, *Konbu-Dashi* (Extract of Kelp)

Rice wine (*Sake*)

27

(continued from page 25)
dipping sauce which is put on sushi just before the sushi is eaten, in addition to being used as a seasoning. There are Japanese-made and Chinese-made soy sauce on the market, both coming in a variety of types. Common Japanese thick soy sauce is suitable for sushi because of its taste and flavor. Some shops use soy sauce as it is as dipping sauce. At my own shop, I use soy sauce as dipping sauce after adding water to soy sauce at a ratio of 1 to 10, boiling and then allowing it to cool. This is done to make soy sauce soft to the palate. Even when sushi is served after cooled *nikiri* (a boiled-down mixture of soy sauce and *mirin* at a ratio of 10 to 3) has been applied to the *tane*, dipping sauce is also used.

### *Nigiri*-Zushi and Tea
Today, sushi shops offer many kinds of drinks, including Japanese *sake*, beer, whisky, wine in addition to Japanese tea. However, formerly they did not serve any drinks other than Japanese tea. The kind of tea that was served was *kona-cha* (powdered tea like a broken black tea), which was prepared and served in large-sized teacups.

This was not because sushi goes well only with Japanese tea, but due to another more practical reason. In former days, *nigiri*-zushi was eaten on the spot only at outdoor sushi stands. Sushi makers tending sushi shops were very busy, as they had to make sushi for many customers at a time, so that they had no time to warm *sake* and serve it to their customers. Even so customers still wanted something to drink while enjoying sushi, so the sushi makers used *kona-cha* which was easy to handle, and served it in large-sized teacups so that they did not have to keep refilling the customers cups again and again. Even today sushi shops still maintain the tradition of serving tea in these over-sized teacups.

# Tools for Making Sushi

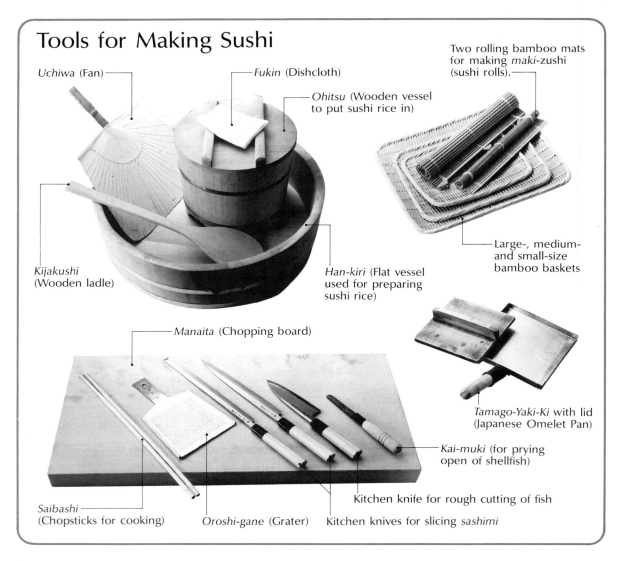

*Uchiwa* (Fan)
*Fukin* (Dishcloth)
*Ohitsu* (Wooden vessel to put sushi rice in)
Two rolling bamboo mats for making *maki*-zushi (sushi rolls).
Large-, medium- and small-size bamboo baskets
*Kijakushi* (Wooden ladle)
*Han-kiri* (Flat vessel used for preparing sushi rice)
*Manaita* (Chopping board)
*Tamago-Yaki-Ki* with lid (Japanese Omelet Pan)
*Kai-muki* (for prying open of shellfish)
Kitchen knife for rough cutting of fish
*Saibashi* (Chopsticks for cooking)
*Oroshi-gane* (Grater)
Kitchen knives for slicing *sashimi*

# The Joy of Sushi

Whatever others may say, the best sushi is *nigiri*-zushi. To know more about sushi is the best way to enjoy it better in a more pleasant atmosphere. As a first step toward achieving this, let's study *nigiri*-zushi thoroughly *tane* by *tane*.

# *Maguro* (Tuna)

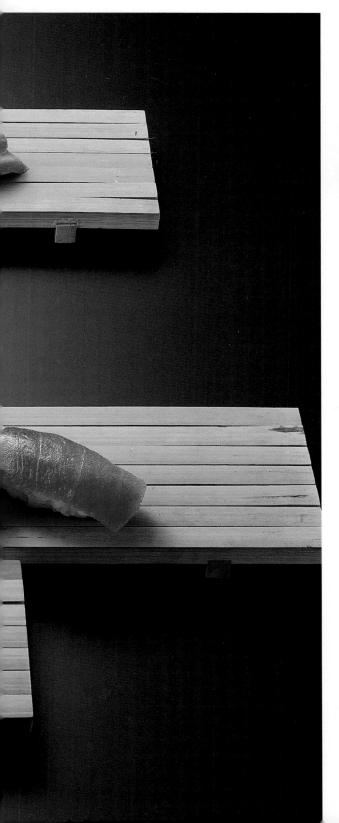

In cases of both lean tuna meat and fatty tuna meat, boiled soy sauce (*nikiri*) is lightly brushed over them before serving to customers. To make boiled soy sauce, add water to soy sauce, boil and let cool. During the old days, this boiled soy sauce was often used on fish in this way. It is far more tasty to eat sushi in this way than just to dip sushi into regular soy sauce. However, even in Japan, the number of sushi shops which use boiled soy sauce has been on the decline.

# What Is *Akami-Dane*?

Sushi makers use the word "*tane*" (or "*dane*" depending on the words that precede it in a word combination) or "sushi-*dane*" to mean the ingredient with which a piece of hand-formed sushi is topped. In contrast to this, the material used for *nori-maki* and *chirashi*-zushi are called "*gu*".

*Tane* are classified roughly into five kinds, according to their nature and the way they are prepared. They are *aka-mi* (red-meat), *shiro-mi* (white-meat), *hikari-mono* (shining *tane*), *nimono* (cooked *tane*), and shrimp, squid, shellfish. We will discuss all those kinds of *tane* later. Here, we will briefly take a look at red-meat *tane*.

Red-meat *tane* include *toro* (oily part of tuna meat), *zuke* (red tuna meat) and bonito meat (see page 49). *Toro* holds a special position among them, without which today's *Edomae*-zushi would be unthinkable. With its soft sweetness and with a taste that melts in your mouth, it is superior to all other forms of sushi-*dane* and may truly called king of all *tane*.

Four kinds of sushi using different parts of tuna. From the bottom of the picture moving up to the top: *akami* (lean tuna meat), *chūtoro* (slightly fatty tuna meat), *ōtoro* (very fatty tuna meat; *shimofuri*, or the meat and fat mixed in such a way as to give a net-type pattern), and *ōtoro* (very fatty tuna meat; *dandara*, or in strips).

# *Maguro* (Tuna)

*Maguro* is the most popular of the *tane* for *Edomae*-zushi and is the most representative of the red-meat *tane*. After it had been regarded as low-class *tane*, first, its red meat came to be praised, and became suddenly popular as the value of its *toro* (fatty meat) came to be recognized as being very delicious. After going through this big change, its position now is unchallenged.

### What is *Toro*?

Today, *maguro* is represented by *toro* (*chū-toro* and *ō-toro*, see illustration on page 33), and it is more popular than its red meat. What is the secret of its unique taste? This secret lies in the fact that the fat of *toro* differs extremely in nature and composition from that of other fish. The fat of the best *toro* is similar in structure to that of marbled beef of the best kind, with many specks of fat spread uniformly throughout its meat. Its taste is mellow with good body to it. It is said to "melt" in your mouth. This special taste of *toro* is due to the above-mentioned structure of its fat.

### Characteristics and Kinds

In the *Edo* period (17th–19th C.), *maguro* was regarded as low quality fish. It is said that *maguro* came to be used as sushi-*dane* for the first time about 140 to 150 years ago. It has made a big contribution to the development of *Edomae* hand-formed sushi. For about 50 to 60 years from the time when it was first used as sushi-*dane*, *maguro* was soaked in soy sauce for some time before served. It was mostly *akami* (red meat of *maguro*), less oily than the other parts, that was used, and in those days *toro* had hardly any market value. The way to prepare *maguro* by soaking in soy sauce was called "*zuke*" at that time, which now means not only the way of preparing *maguro* but also red-meat tuna (*akami*) itself prepared in this way.

There are more than 10 tuna varieties that are called *maguro* at sushi shops, if swordfish and other fish used as substitutes for tuna are included. Outlined below are the characteristics and the taste of some of them.

● *Kuro-Maguro* (Tuna)——This is also called *shibi-maguro* and *hon-maguro*, and is thought to be the best for sushi-*dane*. It is called this because the skin of its back is black (*kuro*). Characteristically, it has short pectoral fins. Its season is in winter and its taste deteriorates remarkably in summer. As might be expected from the fact that it is the king among the different varieties of tuna, a fully grown tuna can be 10 feet (3 m) and weight as much as 900 pounds (400 kg). A tuna weighing about 400 to 450 pounds (180 to 200 kg) is considered to be the best for sushi-*dane*. The meat is darkish-red in color. As the amount of tuna being caught has sharply decreased, it has become extremely expensive.

Its young are called *meji* and those in the middle of their growth are referred to as *nakaboushi*. *Nakaboushi* is a very convenient sushi-*dane*, as its meat is not so light as that of *meji*, nor is it so oily as fully grown tuna.

● *Mebachi* (Bigeye Tuna)——It is very large with big eyes. Its skin is thinner than that of tuna, with the meat which is ½ to 1 inch (1 to 2 cm) from the skin giving off a rather peculiar, obnoxious smell. This part of the meat is always discarded. The meat is bright red, consisting mainly of red meat. It is soft and fairly tasty, but the demerit of this fish is that it is a little sticky. However, if the meat is very fresh, it is not sticky at all. The season is in spring. *Mebachi* grows to a length of about 7 feet (2 m).

● *Kihada* (Yellow-Skinned Tuna)——It is "yellow-skinned *maguro*" because its side skin and fins are yellowish in color. Its second dorsal fin and anal fin are remarkably long and large. The meat is pinkish and firm. Its season is in summer and autumn when tuna is out of season. Fully grown *kihada* is 5 to 10 feet (1.5 to 3 m) in length, and 450 pounds (200 kg) at the maximum in weight.

● *Minami-Maguro* (Southern Tuna, Indian Tuna) and Atlantic *Maguro*——*Minami-maguro* looks very much like tuna, and its meat is the oiliest of all varieties of tuna meat. Thanks to the development of refrigeration technology, it has come to hold an important place as far as frozen *maguro* meat is concerned. It is caught extensively in the southern hemisphere. Its meat varies in quantity of fat and deteriorates in quality according to the area where it is caught. So when buying, it is better to know where it has been caught. In recent years, Atlantic *maguro* caught in the Atlantic Ocean off New York on the 40th Parallel has come to attract a great deal of attention, because the color of its meat is fine and the meat is fatty. It stands midway between *kuro-maguro* and *minami-maguro*.

● *Kajiki* (Swordfish) and Its Varieties——*Kajiki* belongs to a different family that of tuna, but it is a high quality fish which has long been used for sushi-*dane* as a substitute for tuna. The meat is beautiful pinkish or bright red in color, and is less fatty than tuna meat. It is very valuable in summer when tuna is out of season.

### How to Prepare

Unlike other fish, as sushi-*dane*, tuna is seldom bought as a whole fish. Different cut off portions—the dorsal portion and the ventral portion—of tuna without the head or tail are sold in the marketplace.

After having bought a portion of tuna meat, you have to remove the blood from it. By "blood-removing" is meant to clean the surface of the meat of blood and also of meat pigment with running water. This process is effective for keeping the color of the meat bright red. After washing it with running water, wipe off the water on the meat with a dishcloth and keep it in a refrigerator.

As for cutting the meat into slices, please refer to the photos below. Generally speaking, the slices of tuna, bonito and other red-meat *tane* are thicker than that of white-meat *tane*, though, of course, care must be taken to make sure that they balance with sushi rice. As the red meat is very soft, it would be too soft to the palate and the taste would be too light unless it is cut in thick slices.

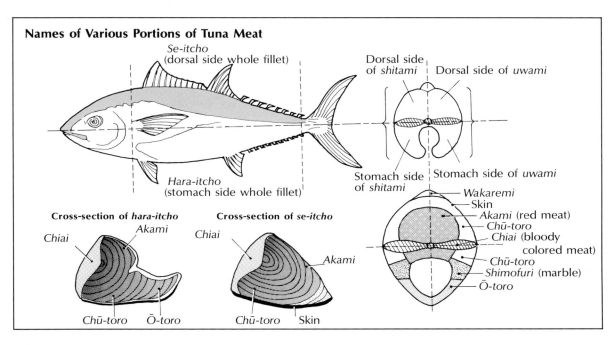

**Names of Various Portions of Tuna Meat**

*Se-itcho* (dorsal side whole fillet)

Dorsal side of *shitami* | Dorsal side of *uwami*

*Hara-itcho* (stomach side whole fillet)

Stomach side of *shitami* | Stomach side of *uwami*

**Cross-section of *hara-itcho***
Chiai — Akami
Chū-toro — Ō-toro

**Cross-section of *se-itcho***
Chiai — Akami
Chū-toro — Skin

Wakaremi
Skin
Akami (red meat)
Chū-toro
Chiai (bloody colored meat)
Chū-toro
Shimofuri (marble)
Ō-toro

**The Method "*Sakudori*" and of Cutting Tuna Meat** (in the case of the stomach side-whole slice—*hara-itcho*)

① The stomach side-whole slice (*hara-itcho*) is cut sideways into three portions each to the width of three "*take*."

② With the skin side down, remove the sinews and bone at the edge of *chiai*, and then remove *chiai*.

③ Make cuts at the ends of the sinews and membrane in the upper half, and cut them off from the meat.

④ After removing *tempa* (upper part), slice the meat horizontally to a thickness of about 1 inch (2.5 cm).

⑤ Continue to slice the meat as explained in ④ until the thickness of the meat from the skin side below is equal to 1 *take*.

⑥ Trim the ends of the meat with the skin and with height of 1 *take*. Slice the meat in widths of about 1 inch (2.5 cm).

⑦ Slice the meat as much as needed as explained in ⑥, and cut off any skin left after the meat has been sliced off.

⑧ Cut the slices into sushi-*dane*, being cut in the direction which is against, not parallel to the sinews.

\* *Take* means a length of meat sufficient for making of one sushi-*dane*, which is about equal to the length of four fingers from the forefinger to the little finger.

# *Tai* (Sea Bream)

# *Hiramasa* (Amber Jack)
# *Suzuki* (Sea Bass)

# *Tai* (Sea Bream)

Sea Bream (*Tai*), together with flatfish, are one of the most popular of the white-meat fish used for sushi. *Tai* are often referred to as the king of fish by the Japanese people. This delicate tasting fish is indispensable at parties and celebrations of all types.

**Characteristics**  More than 100 varieties of *tai* exist in Japan, but the majority of them are really not *tai* in the true sense. Only about 10 varieties (taxonomically) belong to the Sparidae family, which include *madai, chidai, kidai, hirekodai, kirenko, hedai, kurodai* and *kichinu*. Unlike the fish used as a substitute for *tai*, real *tai* have 11 to 13 bones making up their dorsal fin together with well developed molar teeth. Among the above listed fish those from *madai* to *kirenko* make up the red variety. *Chidai* and *hirekodai* are of the bloody dark-red type. The yellowish-red varieties are *kidai* and *kirenko*. *Madai* has a pinkish color with a black-ridged tail fin and dark-blue spots above its eyes.

*Madai* is extraordinary as an ingredient for sushi. Especially, *Akashidai* and *Narutodai*, which are caught in the Seto Inland Sea, are famous and are said to have high commercial value due to their superb taste.

Actually, in sushi shops throughout Japan, the fish which are similar to but not really *tai* are being used extensively. Examples of these types are *ishidai* and *matoudai*.

**Season and Taste**  *Tai* are special in that they have a plain and elegant taste as well as being very light to the palate. They are very high in protein and low in fat when compared to the other types of fish. One thing that is especially good about this type of fish is that it can keep its taste for a much longer period of time than most fish, since the enzyme in the meat is low, causing it to deteriorate at much slower rate.

It is worth mentioning that the head of this fish is edible, and the eyeballs are an especially rich source of Vitamin B$_1$, although these two are not really related to the preparation of sushi.

When ranked according to popularity and taste, *madai* stands out above all others and is followed by *chidai, kidai, hirekodai* and *hedai* in that order.

Most are of the opinion that *tai* are delicious all year round, with the taste dropping a little after the spawning season. At this time, they are referred to as *mugiwaradai* (straw bream).

*Madai* has its spawning season from April to June, and thought to be at its peak during the winter season. *Chidai* spawns from September to November, being at its best from spring to summer. As the season for *Chidai* is opposite that of *madai*, *chidai* is often eaten in summer as a substitute for *madai*. *Kidai, hedai* and *kichinu* spawn in April to June and are said to be at their best from winter to early spring which is the same as *madai*. *Kurodai* has its spawning season from April to September, with most being caught from summer to autumn, when it is considered to be the most delicious.

*Madai* is capable of reaching a length of 3 feet (1 m) or more, but those ranging from 1⅓ to 2 feet (40 to 60 cm) are said to be the tastiest. There is an old Japanese saying which goes like this, "Sea bream of one *shaku* (approx. 1 foot＝30 cm, measured from the eyes to the tip of the tail) are superior in taste."

The best tasting *tai* are those freshly caught having very lean, tight meat, glossy skin and deep black eyes. Another indication showing that *tai* are fresh is the slightly plump rear portion.

**How to Prepare**  Remove the scales, cut off the head and fillet both sides, discarding the middle, bony section. Cut into 4 fillets and remove the white stringy part and peel off the skin before serving, slicing into thinner slices than you would for tuna.

As the skin of *tai* is exceptionally delicious, it is advisable to leave the skin on for *tai* weighing less than 4 pounds (2 kg).

For those larger than 4 pounds, the skin should be removed since its texture is harder and will spoil the taste of the fish. The fish should be served raw in this case.

*Tai* with its skin still on cannot be served raw, but should be cooked as "yushimo" in the following way. Remove the white stringy part from the skin and salt slightly. Cover with a cloth and pour hot water over it. Dip in cold water and take out immediately. Wipe away any remaining moisture, wrap in a wet cloth and store in the refrigerator.

It should be sliced thin into slices normally used for hand-formed sushi. Since the size of *tai* is smaller than that of such fish as tuna, more rice must be used to make sushi of the same size.

# Hiramasa (Amber Jack)

*Hiramasa* belongs to the amberjack. This white-meat fish is served as top-of-the-line sushi during the summer months. Although it has been used as sushi for 50 to 60 years, it is not well known among the sushi gourmets.

**Characteristics**  *Hiramasa* closely resembles *buri*, being slightly slimmer and larger than *buri*. The yellow band-like stripe running down both its sides has a tone which is deeper and a bit sharper than that of *buri*.

Its slimmer body and color contrast remarkably from *kanpachi*. The yellow band-like stripe covering its sides is much clearer. As it cannot be caught in great quantities as opposed to *kanpachi*, it is not often available, although it is valued highly as a sushi *tane*.

Like *kanpachi*, it spawns much later than *buri* in May through August. A fully grown *hiramasa* will reach a length of 5 feet (1.5 m).

**Season and Taste**  *Hiramasa* is most delicious in early summer. The reason why this delicate meat is rated so high is because it is light to the palate, being less fatty than *buri*.

*Hiramasa* up to 3 feet (1 m) in length is considered to be the most delicious. Beyond 3 feet (1 m), the meat of this fish decreases in taste as it increases in length.

**How to Prepare**  Fillet both sides, discarding the middle, bony section in the same way as was done with *kanpachi* (see page 40). Cut into 4 fillets and remove the white stringy part. Peel off the skin and slice into slices thinner than you would normally slice fish of the red-meat type.

# Suzuki (Sea Bass)

Suzuki is a white-meat fish with a taste similar to *kanpachi, hiramasa* and *shima-aji. Suzuki* is the top of its class as a white-meat fish during the summer months, the same as *tai* (sea bream) and *hirame* (flatfish) are during winter season.

**Characteristics**  It is a very strong and masculine-looking fish in appearance. Its smart appearance often resembles that of *tai* and *katsuo*.

The top half is brownish from dorsal fin to tail. When alive it has a golden luster with its stomach section having a silvery-shiny texture to it. This large-boned fish, having an exceptionally strong shape from its large and small dorsal fins to its tail, is a fish of great power.

Its name changes as it grows, making *suzuki* one of *shusse-uo* (ascending fish). It is called *koppa* by people in and around Tokyo when it is about 2 inches (5 to 6 cm), *seigo* when about 1 foot (20 to 30 cm), *fukko* when 1 to 2 feet (30 to 60 cm) and *suzuki* when it becomes larger than 2 feet (60 cm). It takes 3 to 4 years to reach its full size. *Seigo* and those larger in size are river migrators making their way up the river between spring and autumn, returning back down again in October.

It spawns during the winter months. A fully grown *suzuki* can reach a length of as much as 3 feet (1 m).

**Season and Taste**  *Suzuki* is the best tasting during the hot, summer season, dropping in taste as winter approaches during which time it spawns.

It has beautifully white meat, very tight and plain in taste. Although plain in taste, it does have a flavor which is unique to this fish. *Suzuki* caught in Shinji Lake, Shimane Prefecture, Western Japan, is said to be the most delicious.

*Suzuki* is one of the most famous fish in Japan, and one of the most popular fish used as a sushi-*dane* especially in summer, because of its freshness and special taste.

**How to Prepare**  Fillet both sides, discarding the middle, bony section. Cut into 4 fillets and remove the white stringy part. Peel off the skin, and cut into thin slices.

As *suzuki* is very fresh, it may be made into *arai* before forming into sushi.

To make *arai*, slice *suzuki* and put these slices in ice-cold water. Stir until sliced meat shrinks giving a wrinkled appearance. The slices become pure white and plain as their fat content is decreased.

*Sumiso* (vinegar and bean paste) is used to give *arai* its special, sophisticated taste.

# Kanpachi (Yellowtail)   Shima-Aji
# Hirame (Flounder)   (Yellow Jack)

# *Buri* (Yellowtail)
# *Kisu* (Sillago)

## What Is *Shiromi-Dane*?

About 10 kinds of fish are used as *shiromi-dane* (white-meat *tane*) today, including sea bream, flounder, sea bass, amber jack, yellow jack (hard-tail), and yellowtail. Of these, the most important are sea bream (especially, red sea bream) and flounder.

White-meat fish is generally treated as high-class sushi-*dane*, and its light and refined flavor is specially cherished by sushi-lovers. It is low in oil content and may be said to be a low calorie sushi-*dane*.

In contrast to the sweetness of oily red-meat and the harmonized flavor of vinegar and oil which is unique to shining *tane*, the white-meat *tane* is loved for its attractive white color and refreshening flavor.

Sea bream and flounder make ideal white-meat *tane*, and hold a special place among sushi-*dane* for their delicate flavor and the pleasant feeling they give to the palate.

*Kanpachi* (upper left), *Buri* (upper right), *Shima-Aji* (center), *Hirame* (lower left), *Kisu* (lower right)

# Kanpachi (Yellowtail, a kind of)

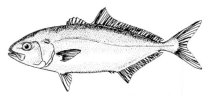

It is only in recent years that this fish has come to be used as sushi-*dane*, becoming popular only after World War II. It is an excellent quality and expensive summer white-meat *tane* for sushi. Normally not oily, but in summer, the body becomes firmer with its meat being oilier, thus having more flavor.

**Characteristics**   Its shape resembles *buri* (yellowtail) but it is flatter and a bit bigger. It is purplish in color and the yellow stripe running lengthwise along the body is darker than *buri*. A fully grown *kanpachi*, can reach a length of 7 feet (2 m). Their spawning season extends from June to August.

**Season and Taste**   Kanpachi is in season from early to mid-summer. As summer white-meat *tane*, it is first-class but the problem is that the amount that can be caught each year is not enough to satisfy demand. Recently, however, fish-farm grown *kanpachi* of good quality is available throughout the year. *Kanpachi* allowed to grow too big has a definite loss in flavor. A 2 to 3 year-old fish of about 2½ feet (80 cm) in length and 10 pounds (5 kg) in weight is considered to be the most delicious. There is only about 0.05 ounce (1.2

g) of fat for 4 ounces (100 g) of *kanpachi*, an amount which is considered to be extremely small.

It is worthy to note that some part of the *Kanpachi*'s meat gives out a bad smell after the spawning season is over, but there is no way of knowing this until gutted and filleted. Therefore, it is better not to use *kanpachi* in early autumn.

**How to Prepare**   Cut off the head and fillet the meat away from the central bone, first along one side of the bone, from head to tail, then turning fish over, fillet along the other side, discarding bony section. Then, cut each filleted piece lengthwise into 2 pieces, a total of 4 pieces altogether. When removing the scales, do not use a scale remover. Use instead a knife (a slender-blade *sashimi* knife provides the best results) and slice the scales thinly away, the same as in a shining fish.

# Buri (Yellowtail)

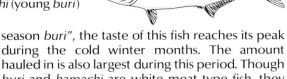

Up to the 1920s, *buri* was a popular fish eaten extensively throughout Japan. It began to be used as sushi-*dane* after World War II and became even more popular as fish-farm grown *hamachi* (young *buri*) became available.

**Characteristics**   This is one of the so-called "popular" fish with its name changing according to its growth stage. The naming of this fish also differs in each region. For example, in Tokyo, a fry is called *Mojako*, those up to 6 inches (15 cm) in length *wakashi*, about 1⅓ feet (40 cm) *inada*, about 2 feet (60 cm) *warasa*, and over 3 feet (90 cm) *buri*, a full-grown fish. In recent years, cultivation has become popular and fish-farm grown *hamachi* of about 1⅓ feet (40 cm) in length is now available on the market throughout the year. It has a rather spindle shape with a yellow stripe running along its sides. Fully grown, it can reach a length of 3 feet (1 m). Its spawning season is in spring.

**Season and Taste**   As there is even a phrase, "cold

season *buri*", the taste of this fish reaches its peak during the cold winter months. The amount hauled in is also largest during this period. Though *buri* and *hamachi* are white-meat type fish, they are oily-type and can be used as a substitute for *toro* (oiliest part of tuna).

**How to Prepare**   Cut the head off and fillet the meat away from the center bone, first along one side of the bone, from head to tail, then turning the fish over, fillet the other side and throw away the bony section. Then, cut each filleted portion into 2 pieces, which will yield a total of 4 pieces. The pylorus (gut part of the fish between stomach and intestines) is very delicious but be sure to remove it as it may cause poisoning.

# Shima-Aji (Yellow Jack)

Among the *aji* family, it is one of the most delicious. It is an excellent-quality and expensive summer white-meat *tane* for sushi. Like *kanpachi*, it became popular as sushi-*dane* only after World War II.

**Characteristics**   Its body is big with a shape resembling *madai* (sea bream). The mouth is big and its lower lip does not protrude out like *ma-aji*. A yellow stripe runs lengthwise along the body and the body color is somewhat like that of *buri*. There is *zengo* on the yellow stripe near the tail.

*Zengo* is a kind of a scale texture characteristic of certain *aji* varieties. It has a scale pattern similar to that of shark's and, in ichthyology (study of fish), it is called "*Junrin*". A fully grown fish reaches a length of about 3 feet (1 m). Its spawning season extends from June to July.

**Season and Taste**    Very little difference in taste can be seen throughout the year, but it is said to be tastiest in June just before the spawning season. Those reaching their maximum size lack the taste of the smaller ones. Those about 1⅓ to 2 feet (40 to 60 cm) in length are said to be good, with those around 1⅓ feet (40 cm) being the most delicious.

**How to Prepare**    Cut off heads and fillet from the center bone, first along one side of the bone, from head to tail, then turning the fish over, fillet the other side and throw away the bony section. Then, cut each filleted portion into 2 pieces, providing a total of 4 pieces. In case of *shima-aji*, be sure to peel off the skin as thinly as possible. Otherwise, the beautiful glossy surface of the fish will be lost.

# Hirame (Flounder)

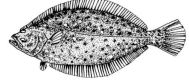

Together with *tai* (sea bream), *hirame* is a typical white-meat type *tane*. Many years ago, *hirame* was able to be caught in Tokyo Bay. It was so tasty that it became sort of a "symbol" of all *Edomae* fish (fish caught in Tokyo Bay).

**Characteristics**    Its shape is flat, with eyes on the left side of its body and having a rather large mouth. The side of the body with the eyes is brownish-black in color and covered with ctenoid scales. The other side is white, and being covered with cycloid scales. It prefers living in the sand on the ocean's bottom eye side up. It is a fish capable of camouflaging itself, thus it can change its body color according to the color of the surrounding sand. Its lateral lines, jaws and teeth are identically developed on both sides. A fully grown *hirame* ranges in length from 2 to 2⅔ feet (60 to 80 cm). The spawning season for this fish is from February to June.

**Season and Taste**    Of all flounder and flatfish found around Japan, this fish is considered to be the most delicious of its kind. It is in season during the winter time, from September to the following February, prior to the beginning of its spawning season. The taste of the fish changes according to its fat content. This fish contains very little fat which makes it light. It is often referred to as "cold season *hirame*," for it is especially tasty during the cold, mid-winter season. However, summer *hirame* cannot come close to matching its winter taste and it is said that "not even a cat eats *hirame* in the summer". However, *hirame* up to around 1⅓ feet (40 cm) in length (called *soge*) is fairly delicious until April or May. As long as it is fresh, with only a slight amount of fat, it can be used as sushi-*dane*. *Engawa* (meat around the fins) of flounder and flatfish is the most delicious part and can be used as expensive sushi-*dane*.

**How to Prepare**    Cut each filleted portion into 2 pieces. Make a little cut around the *engawa* both top and bottom beforehand, and slice these parts off after the filleted parts have been cut in half. This will yield a total of 4 long pieces together with 4 *engawa*.

To slice these pieces as sushi-*dane*, cut thinly, the same as with *tai*, from the tail end. As for the *engawa*, if it is large enough, slice it about the length of each *nigiri* and hand-form with rice. If it is small, slice about the length of *nigiri* but use 2 slices, overlapping them, and hand-form with rice.

# Kisu (Sillago)

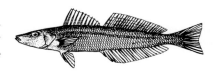

The skin of fresh *kisu* has a beautiful golden shine to it. It is this "shining" sushi-*dane* that we cannot do without during the hot summer months. *Sayori, kasugo* (or *kodai*), and *kisu* are considered the three best "shining" *tane*.

**Characteristics**    Though there are two kinds of kisu, *shirogisu* (white sillago) and *aogisu* (blue sillago), with the one used as sushi-*dane* is *shirogisu*. This fish prefers living in the sand in clear water, either along coast or bay area. It is a slender and roundish in shape. It has a back of a golden light ash color with its stomach being silvery white. The glossy skin makes it look very graceful and beautiful. The spawning season is from August to September.

**Season and Taste**    This fish is in season from June to July but there is not much difference in taste throughout the year. As it is called the "*ayu* of the ocean", its taste is light and refined, much more than *sayori*, and is just perfect as sushi-*dane*. It has only an extremely small amount of fat. Care must be taken as its taste deteriorates very quickly once caught, so it must be served as fresh as possible.

**How to Prepare**    Cut fish open from the back side, butterfly style, and let soak in vinegar for a while. Those which are very fresh can be served raw after the skin is removed. When using, cut the butterflied *kisu* in half at the center along its stomach. If it happens to be small, use the whole piece. As the body of *kisu* is slender, make an opening cut on the thick part of fillet and use it.

# *Kohada* (Gizzard Shad)

# *Kasugo* (Young Sea Bream)
# *Sayori* (Halfbeak)

## What Is *Hikari-Mono*?

While a descriptions is given regarding *maguro, katsuo* (to be described later) as red-meat fish (red-meat *tane*), and *tai, suzuki, kanpachi,* and *hirame* as white-meat *tane*, there is still another group of important sushi-*dane* which is collectively referred to as "*hikari-mono*" (shining fish as sushi-*dane*).

Examples of this group are *kohada, kasugo (kodai), sayori, kisu* (p. 41), *aji* and *saba*. Common features and position among sushi-*dane* of *hikari-mono* are given on top of next page prior to explaining each of these types of fish.

## Features and Position of *Hikari-Mono*

*Hikari-mono* are small fish with a shining dorsal skin, which are used for sushi toppings by seasoning with salt and vinegar with the skin left intact.

Position of *hikari-mono* among hand-formed sushi (*nigiri-zushi*) is such an absolutely necessity that it would be reduced to half if *hikari-mono* were to be excluded. Since *hikari-mono* require a great deal of the skill and experience, it is said that the skill of a sushi shop can be evaluated by the *hikari-mono* it serves.

View from the aspect of taste, the meat situated in the middle between the rich red meat and plain white meat is the part providing a refreshing sensation to the palate.

## *Kohada* (Gizzard Shad)

The king of *hikari-mono* (shining-type fish). When one talks about *hikari-mono*, *kohada* is now thought to be number one. However, it was regarded 40 years ago as the lowest among *hikari-mono* and was not used as *tane* for high-class sushi, probably due to its undeserved reputation.

**Characteristics**   *Kohada* is a fish common throughout Tokyo. Its scientific name is *konoshiro*. It belongs to the group of the ascending fish (*shusse-uo*), which is called *shinko* when it is about 2 inches (5 to 6 cm) in length, *kohada* when 5 inches (12 to 13 cm), *nakatsumi* when 7 inches (16 to 17 cm), and *konoshiro* when it reaches a mature size of 8 inches (20 cm) or larger. It is said that the meat is most delicious when it is of the *kohada* size.

*Kohada* belongs to the same family as herring and mackerel but is rather flat and thin. It is characterized by the long, soft thread-like pattern extending from the last dorsal fin. Lateral strings of black dots against a blue-silvery shiny background greatly contribute to its beautiful appearance. It spawns from spring to summer. A fully grown *kohada* (*konoshiro*) will reach an average length of about 10 inches (25 cm).

**Season and Taste**   In autumn when *shinko* begins to appear in the market, it lacks the thick fatty taste, having a rather plain taste with hidden richness. It is thought to be best tasting in November when the fish grows to the *kohada* size with an adequate proportion of fat and this lasts until February of the next year, making *kohada* popular as "*hikari-mono* in winter". *Konoshiro*, as the fish is called in April, is less frequently used as it is too large for sushi-*dane*. As mentioned already, in winter, when it is called *kohada*, is the best season for use as sushi-*dane*. However, this yearly change in the taste is disappearing as *kohada* is now being served all year round.

**How to Prepare**   The cooking of *kohada* provides the basis for the preparation of all other kinds *hikari-mono*. If a sushi shop does not properly prepare *kohada*, the sushi shop will be thought of as lacking in their preparation of other sushi-*dane*.

Remove the head first, then slice open the stomach to discard any bones and guts. Seasoning of the meat with salt and vinegar is the most common way of preparing the various kinds of *hikari-mono*. The way in which this seasoning is applied will govern the final taste of sushi.

● *Furishio* (Salting)——Sprinkle salt evenly over the surface of a flat plate or bamboo basket. Place the opened *kohada* meat with the skin-side down without overlapping or leaving any space and sprinkle salt from over it again. To make a large number of *kohada*, place them over the already salted *kohada* as previously mentioned and sprinkle with salt. Repeat this process with care so as to spread the salt evenly.

The most important point is how long they are salted, time before they are rinsed off with water. The general rule of thumb is to salt for a short time during warm weather and for a long time during the cold season, but this varies to a considerable extent from shop to shop. Generally, 1 to 1.5 hours in summer and 3 to 4 hours in coldest days of winter. This also depends upon the size and fat content of the fish. The most commonly used method is to spread the salt over the fish, allowing it to dissove without leaving any dry salt on them.

Rinse quickly once or twice with a large volume of water to remove the salt and surface fat.

● *Suarai* (Rinse with vinegar)——Drain and rinse one by one in vinegar. For rinsing, use the vinegar previously used for seasoning *kohada*. This process is essential to remove any unpleasant taste or fishy smell and to allow the vinegar to penetrate quickly and uniformly in the next step of dipping in vinegar.

● *Tsukekomi* (Dipping in vinegar)——Drain vinegar lightly. Fill a large bowl with fresh vinegar prior to dipping. Lay *kohada* with the skin-side down in a circular form like a chrysanthemum flower. If the bowl is small and the meat has to be placed on top of each other, take care to allow sufficient vinegar penetration into the meat. The volume of vinegar is enough when all fish meat is sufficiently covered. They are seasoned adequately when their surface begins to turn white, for about 15 to 20 minutes for *kohada*.

Then, remove from the vinegar, stack and allow the vinegar to drain. Leaving *kohada* to drain for half a day will result in the best taste.

The above process is seasoning with salt and vinegar. *Kohada* may be served as sushi-*dane*

without slicing (*maruzuke*), or cutting into two (*katami*, half a fish) or three slices (⅓ fish). Two pieces of whole *shinko* are used to top a hand-formed sushi as they are small. Make shallow cutting marks on the hard surface of the skin in all cases.

# *Kasugo* (Young Sea Bream)

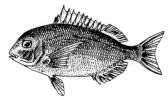

*Kasugo*, young sea bream, together with *sayori* and *kisu*, is counted among the three most delicious of the delicate tasting shining *tane*. However, it is not seen so much today due to the popularity of *kohada*.

**Characteristics**    *Kasugo* is the name given to young sea bream in Tokyo and is most commonly known as *kodai*. Sea bream takes about three years to reach its mature size. *Kasugo* is a sea bream only about one year old, not yet capable of spawning, and measures just 4 inches (10 cm) in length. It is evaluated as one of the best in high quality *tane* among the shining *tane*, presumably related to the fact that sea bream, especially full-size ones, are particularly cherished by the Japanese.

**Season and Taste**    One very commonly accepted theory regarding "season" is that fish are the most delicious just before spawning, but *kasugo* which is not capable of spawning, has no season at all. Furthermore, the spawning periods of various types of sea bream differ to some extent so that

one-year old *kasugo* are available on the market throughout the year. In other words, each different district has its own "season" for *kasugo*. As for the taste of *kasugo*, it may be said that its taste is more delicate than that of fully grown sea bream, having a taste which is lighter and more refined.

**How to Prepare**    Open the fish from the backbone and remove the center bone, but always leave the tail intact. The tail can be cut into two portions, so that if you use each side of it, you can make two sushi topped with a tail-having *tai*.

Season with salt and vinegar in the same way as *kohada*. Take care to dip the *tane* by folding the sides with their outer sides facing one another so as to keep the skin glossy and the tail in good shape.

# *Sayori* (Halfbeak)

This is the most highly valued of all the spring shining *tane*. Its season follows that of *kohada* and precedes that of *kisu* and *aji*. With its elegant shape and style, it is compared to a daughter of gentle birth, and ranks high among the shining *tane* being served in sushi shops.

**Characteristics**    *Sayori* is a sea fish, but it has the habit of going up rivers. It is generally flat and long, and its body excepting its stomach side is covered with round-shaped scales. It has a protruding lower jaw, and the lower jaw of a male *sayori* becomes red. Like a flying fish, it sometimes jumps above the surface of the water. The spawning period is from May through July. A fully grown *sayori* is about 1⅓ feet (40 cm) in length.

**Season and Taste**    It is in season from March to April. In particular, *sayori* in early spring is highly valued. *Sayori* in autumn, however, is not bad at all. The meat is white and has a delicate smell, and though its taste may seem at first to be light, actually it is a little on the heavy side. As compared with other shining *tane*, *sayori*, like *kisu* and *kasugo*, is less oily. Once it loses its freshness, it soon becomes stale. Take care if the color of the stomach part turns from silvery white to brown. The brighter the red color of the lower jaw, the fresher it is.

**How to Prepare**    Fillet from the stomach side. *Sayori* is a shapely fish, but its entrails are blackish and dirty-looking, so make sure to wash away all the entrails to get clean, fresh-looking fillets.

Sprinkle with salt and wash off with vinegar in the same way as you would with *kohada*. Allow the salt to set for about 20 minutes during the warm season, and about 30 minutes during the cold season. In order to keep the skin of this fish as glossy as possible during the time it is being washed in vinegar, fold large *sayori* with the outer sides inside and pile small *sayori* one upon the other, with their backs facing one another. This procedure should also be followed when dipping them in vinegar. Dipping time ranges from 2 to 3 minutes. It is better to finish vinegar-dipping a little earlier than you may think fit.

*Sayori* is one of the easiest fish to prepare. The cutting of this fish can be done in many different ways when being used as sushi-*dane*. *Oboro* may be used to give it additional flavor.

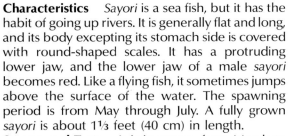

# *Aji* (Horse Mackerel)
# *Saba* (Mackerel)

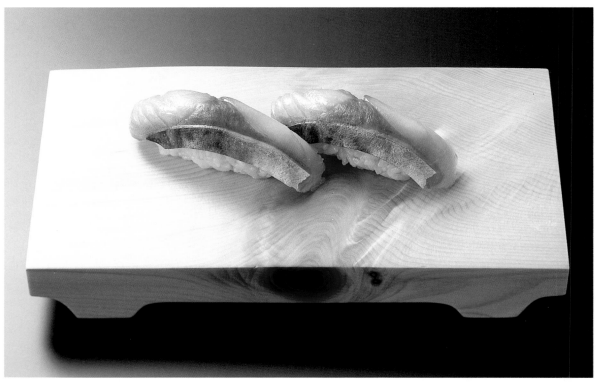

# *Iwashi* (Sardine)
# *Katsuo* (Bonito)

# *Aji* (Horse Mackerel)

*Aji* is representative shining *tane* from late spring to summer. While *kisu* is high-class shining *tane* in summer, *aji* is a popular one. Today, *kohada* is very popular, but in the past *aji* held the number one position during the summer season.

**Characteristics**    There are many varieties of *aji*. *Ma-aji* is the type used as shining *tane* at sushi shops. This kind of *aji* is caught in the largest quantities. There are two different kinds of *aji* living in the coastal waters of Japan. One kind inhabits the bay areas, while the other migrates offshore. The former is called *ki-aji* because its back has a pale yellow color, while the latter is called *kuro-aji* because its back is blackish-blue. More *kuro-aji* are caught than *ki-aji*, but the latter's taste is much better. Common to all varieties of *aji*, it has "zengo" (prickly scales; see *shima-aji* on page 40), which run clearly from the head to the tail part in the central part of the body in a curve. The spawning season is from April to July. A fully grown *aji* can reach a length of 1⅓ feet (40 cm).

**Season and Taste**    *Aji* is tasty throughout the year, but is considered to be at its best during the summer months. The meat is not so oily and there is nothing peculiar about its taste, so that it is loved by all people. For sushi-*dane*, it is better to use small- or medium-sized *aji* so that the whole one-side fillet may be used for one sushi.

**How to Prepare**    First, completely remove the "zengo". To remove *zengo* is the most basic technique for professional beginners. Use a small- or medium-sized *deba* knife. Place a fish on its side and lay the knife on it, moving it to and fro lightly, removing the *zengo* starting from the tail section. Take care not to cut into the skin or meat.

Then, cut the fish open from the back and salt it for about 30 minutes. To soak in vinegar, fold the meat with the skin sides inside as in the case of *sayori*. It should be allowed to soak in vinegar for about 10 minutes.

Usually, in serving *aji* as sushi-*dane*, the meat is cut into two pieces along the stomach line, and one-side fillet is used. Peel off only the thin skin, leaving the lower silvery skin.

Recently, *aji* is being served raw. In this case, fillet the two sides of the fish from the center bone, and make cuts in the fillets along the line on the skin, and serve it, topping it with minced chives and grated ginger.

# *Saba* (Mackerel)

Kyoto has been noted for its *saba*-zushi, which is a kind of *bō*-zushi of the *nare*-zushi type, and so *saba* is said to be a representative fish for *Kansai*-zushi. Until about 60 years ago, *saba* was also popular in Tokyo, but it does not enjoy such popularity as it once did.

**Characteristics**    *Saba* is one of fish whose yearly haul is the largest, and is very popular throughout Japan. There are two varieties of *saba* that are used as sushi-*dane*, that is, *ma-saba* (also called *hon-saba* and *hira-saba*) and *goma-saba* (or *maru-saba*). The former has a glossy, beautiful blue wavy pattern along its dorsal part, with a silvery white stomach. The latter has less of a regular wavy pattern, and has spots the size of a red bean on its sides and smaller spots the size of sesame seeds on its stomach. The cross-section of the middle part of the latter's body is more roundish than that of the former. *Ma-saba* is far more important as sushi-*dane* than *goma-saba*, which is used as a substitute for *ma-saba* in the summer season when the taste of *ma-saba* deteriorates.

The spawning season is from February through August for *ma-saba* and from May through July for *goma-saba*. A fully grown *saba* reaches a length about 1½ feet (45 cm). *Ma-saba* grows somewhat larger than *goma-saba*.

**Season and Taste**    *Ma-saba* is in season in autumn, and it is particularly tasty in late autumn when its meat is more oily. So much so that there is a proverb in Japan which says, "Do not let your wife eat autumn *saba*." Spring *saba* and summer *saba* are less oily and more watery. *Goma-saba* is available on the market throughout the year, but its taste is best in autumn. *Saba* has its own unique taste, which is due to the fact that its meat contains a kind of histidine, an amino acid, which is the tasty component of the red meat of *maguro*, *katsuo* and other red-meat fish.

**How to Prepare**    There is an old saying which says, "*Saba* becomes stale even while it is living." What it is actually saying is that *saba* is one fish that has a tendency to deteriorate very quickly. This is due to the fact that it has a strong enzyme which causes self-digestion after cadaveric stiffening. The main point in preparing *saba* is, therefore, to select *saba* as fresh as possible and to prepare it quickly and properly.

After cutting it open, butterfly style, prepare it like you would in the case of *kohada*. Salt it for about 2 to 3 hours and soak it in vinegar for 1 to 1.5 hours.

# Iwashi (Sardine)

It is only recently that sardines came to be used as sushi-*dane*. It is said that in former days sushi makers relished them privately.

**Characteristics**   Sardines are one fish which is very essential to the Japanese table. The only variety of sardines that is used by sushi shops is *ma-iwashi*. It is rather flat, and its beautiful blue color is darker along the dorsal part. There is a row of black spots in the central part of its sides. According to the stages of its growth, it is called *koba-iwashi* (4 inches=10 cm or less), *chūba-iwashi* (4 to 7 inches=10 to 18 cm) and *ōba-iwashi* (7 inches= 18cm or more). The spawning season is from February through March. A fully matured *iwashi* is about 10 inches (25 cm) long.

**Season and Taste**   Sardines are oiliest and considered to be the best tasting in early autumn. Therefore, *ma-iwashi* is also called *aki-iwashi* (au-

tumn *iwashi*). The taste drops off after spawning.

**How to Prepare**   At present, it is served raw in many cases. In order to make it taste best, it is important to serve it after soaking it in vinegar.

Fillet it into two, discarding the center bone, and sprinkle salt over the filleted portions. After salting, allow them to sit for more than 3 hours. After rinsing them in vinegar, soak them in vinegar for 3 to 4 hours. When soaking, use the vinegar that has already been used for any of the other fish. After you have finished soaking them in vinegar, make sure to drain off the vinegar well. Use the fillets after storing them overnight in a refrigerator, if possible. The taste of vinegar will make much more mellow and the meat will taste better.

# Katsuo (Bonito)

Formerly, *katsuo* was not offered by sushi shops, as it was regarded as being unfit for sushi. It has been only since about 20 years ago that it began to be popular as a new sushi-*dane*. It is said to be classed as a red-meat *tane*, but not in the sense that it is used as a substitute for *maguro tane*, but because it is a special raw fish *tane* in its own right.

**Characteristics**   Like *maguro* and *saba*, it belongs to the *saba* family. In Japan it is an important fish, whose meat is widely used in the form of *katsuo-bushi* (dried bonito or its flakes) for *dashi* (see page 70), and *tataki* (a kind of *sashimi*). It is shaped exactly like a spindle, and its cross-section is almost round. It has no scales except on its pectoral fins and the lateral line running from its head to tail, and there are several gray stripes on both sides. It is a strong and powerful swimmer. It spawns in the warm ocean, and the spawning season is believed to be very long. A fully grown *katsuo* measures 2 to 3 feet (60 to 90 cm) in length.

**Season and Taste**   As *katsuo* is a migratory fish and as its spawning season is long, it is difficult to pinpoint its season exactly. However, it is in autumn that *katsuo* becomes oily and its meat becomes full and firm. Since the *Edo* people had a special attachment to "*hatsugatsuo*" (early *katsuo*), people in Tokyo tend to regard *katsuo* as being in season in the April to May period. Actually, however, it is less oily during this season.

*Katsuo* meat is rich in protein, but has a peculiar smell. In order to kill this fishy smell, ginger, chives and onion are used as spices. It is also rich in Vitamin D.

**How to Prepare**   Like *saba*, *katsuo* deteriorates very rapidly. It is absolutely necessary that it should be used on the day on which it is brought to the shop, and should be eaten within 2 to 3 hours after being filleted. Fillet it, and cut each fillet into four

pieces. In case it is eaten raw, remove the skin and cut the pieces into thick slices. The following two ways are recommended.

● *Tosa* Style——It is because of this method that *katsuo* has become a fine sushi-*dane* in recent years. This type of preparation is called "*yaki-shimo*"—meaning to quickly roast the skin of *katsuo* with high heat. This is an application to sushi-making of the "*tataki*" cooking style for which Tosa (Kochi Prefecture) is well known. Like that of *tai*, the skin of *katsuo* is very tasty. By this cooking method, the tasty skin can be retained, and at the same time, its fishy smell can be killed by the aroma of the meat being roasted.

After being roasted using high heat, the meat should be soaked quickly once in vinegar. Cut it into thick slices. Use grated ginger, chives or minced *wakegi* (Japanese onion stems) as spices.

● Soy Sauce Soaking——This is a kind of "*zuke*" cooking (see page 32). Remove the skin and bloody colored-meat from the cut meat, and arrange the meat in a bamboo basket and soak it in soy sauce added an adequate amount of freshly squeezed ginger juice for 4 to 5 hours. After removing the soy sauce from the cut meat as much as possible, slice it. Use Japanese mustard powder dissolved in water instead of *wasabi* (Japanese horseradish) in forming sushi, and spread *nikiri* (boiled soy sauce) over the *tane*. (See page 28).

# *Ebi* (Shrimp)

*Ebi* placed in center are in raw, and called *"odori"*

# *Ika* (Squid, Cuttlefish)
# *Tako* (Octopus)

*Tako* (upper left only). *Ika* placed upper right is in raw, the other *Ika* are boiled.

# Ebi (Shrimp)

*Ebi* is a representative high-class sushi-*dane*. It is usually boiled before being used. However, sometimes live *ebi* (called *odori*, which means dancing) are used as sushi-*dane*. Because of its good taste and its elegant shape, it has been called the king of sushi-*dane* as far back as the *Edo* period (17th–19th C.).

**Kinds and Characteristics**    There are many varieties of shrimp. It is said that they number nearly 2,000. At the same time, the number of varieties that are used as sushi-*dane* has increased recently. Formerly, *ebi* meant *kuruma-ebi* at sushi shops. Today, *hokkoku-akaebi* (*ama-ebi*) and *botan-ebi* have come to be used widely as sushi-*dane*.

● *Kuruma-ebi* (Wheel Shrimp)——Generally speaking, sushi makers do not use the word *kuruma-ebi*. According to its growth stage, *sai-maki* or *ko-maki* (2 inches=5 to 6 cm), *chū-maki* (4 inches=10 cm), *maki* or *kuruma-ebi* (about 6 inches=15 cm) and *ō-guruma* (8 to 10 inches=20 to 25 cm). It is *maki* that is most widely used at sushi shops and which has the best taste. Following it are *chū-maki* and *sai-maki*. In recent years, *maki* is being artificially cultured throughout Japan and is available in the marketplace all the year round. Raw shrimp has dark-brown stripes on the grayish-brown or pale-blue ground. When boiled, it turns into a beautiful red-and-white pattern.

● *Ama-ebi* (Sweet Shrimp)——As the name shows, it tastes very sweet when eaten raw. It is about 4 inches (10 cm) in length. It has a small prickle on the third section of its shell. It is a relative new sushi-*dane* and is served raw.

● *Botan-ebi*——About 6 inches (15 cm) in length, it is pale-red in color and is served raw in almost all cases. It is a high-class sushi-*dane*, and is used only for hand-formed sushi. Each time an order is placed, the sushi maker peels off the shell. It is used almost exclusively in the Tohoku and Hokkaido Districts where it is caught.

**Season and Taste**    Natural *kuruma-ebi* spawns from the end of June through August, and is caught in large quantities in spring and summer. It is seldom caught in winter. Today, cultured *kuruma-ebi* is available throughout the year, and it may be said that it has no special season. Generally speaking, the taste of *kuruma-ebi* does not change so much throughout the year, but it is in late autumn that the meat becomes full, providing the maximum in taste. Its special taste is due to the fact that its meat contains betaine, which provides a light sweetness, and an alginine.

**How to Prepare**    Before boiling, skewer shrimp. Put some salt in boiling water, and dip the shrimp in it. The shrimp float above struggling, and it is said the shrimp are properly boiled when they float. Scoop them up quickly. It takes only about 3 to 4 minutes to boil them. Put soon the boiled shrimp in cold water, and when they are cooled, remove the shell from the shrimp on the skewer. Pull out the skewer, and cut open the shrimp from the stomach side to make "noshi" shrimp.

Today, shrimp are served as they are after being boiled. However, if the following treatment is given shrimp will taste even better.

Soak *noshi* shrimp in water mildly salted for only about 1 to 2 minutes, and wash them by passing them through water and drain off. Lay a dry cloth in a bowl, arrange the shrimp on it with the opened side down, and refrigerate them. Only those shrimp that are necessary are taken out when an order is placed. At this time, soak in sweetened vinegar (add sugar, and if necessary, *mirin* to vinegar) for 1 to 2 minutes, and then place them in a bamboo basket to allow the vinegar to drain off. Then, the shrimp are ready to be served.

In case they are served raw as "odori", dip only the tail of the shrimp in boiling water, to make it turn red. Put them in cold water to cool. In this case, cut open the shrimp from the back side.

As *ama-ebi* have very soft meat, and as the rice is apt to turn red due to the shrimp's red body color, form sushi softly and carefully.

*Botan-ebi* are cut open from the back, and one *botan-ebi* is used for one piece of sushi. The meat of this shrimp is also very soft, so that it is necessary to take care so as not to crush it.

# Ika (Squid, Cuttlefish)

*Ika* was once a *nimono-dane* (see page 63) second in importance only to *anago*. Today, however, it is served raw in almost all cases. Whichever the case, it has long been a very popular *tane*.

**Characteristics**    There are many varieties of *ika*, which are roughly classified into those which have thick outer meat and a thick internal chitinous support, and others which have thin outer meat and a soft, transparent internal support. The former are *kou-ika* or *sumi-ika* and the like, including *mongou-ika* and *shiriyake-ika*, while the latter include *aori-ika*, *yari-ika* and *surume-ika*, which have a cylindrical body pointed at the tip and a triangular caudal fin on each side. However, only *aori-ika* has thick meat and a pair of broad, fan-like round caudal fins. All *ika* have eight short legs and two long legs, each with suckers inside. They also have an ink bag and eject ink when attacked by an enemy.

About 95 percent of *ika* that are served raw as sushi-*dane* are *mongou-ika*, while other varieties of *ika* are tastier as *nimono-dane*.

**Season and Taste**    All the varieties of *ika*, including *mongou-ika*, that are used as sushi-*dane*, are frozen and are available throughout the year, so that it may be said that actually there is no season for *ika*. However, the season for live *ika* is from autumn through winter for *kou-ika* and *mongou-ika*, from spring through summer for *aori-ika*, from late spring through autumn for *yari-ika*, and from early summer through autumn for *surume-ika*. Generally speaking, the meat of *ika* is thinner and the shell is harder after the spawning season. The particular taste of *ika* is due to the fact that the meat contains amino acids having a strong sweetness.

**How to Prepare**    All kinds of *ika* are prepared basically in the same way in the first stage. Wash *ika* as it is in water, remove the shell from *kou-ika* and similar varieties and the cartilage from *surume-ika* and *yari-ika*, and separate *geso* (legs) and the visceral mass from the body. Wash the meat in water and peel off the skin. In peeling off

it, use a cloth so as not to damage the meat.

In case it is served raw, cut off the fringe to shape the meat and slice it. In case it is served as *nimono-dane*, treat the meat as follows.

Put the meat in boiling water with a pinch of salt in it, and turn it quickly using chopsticks for 3 to 4 seconds. In case the meat is about 6 inches (15 cm) in length, adjust the boiling time according to the size of the meat. Then, put it in cold water to cool. The meat has been properly boiled when it is about as hard as one's earlobe.

Heat broth you prepared to a boil and put the meat in. In a few seconds, the meat curls and becomes sufficiently elastic, and the boiling is over in a few seconds after that. The broth is prepared by adding sugar to soy sauce at a ratio of 3 to 10, and adding to it a small amount of water. The amount of the broth need not be large, as water seep out of the meat.

Slice the meat vertically to the muscle fibers of the meat. The muscles of *ika* run sidewise to the longitudinal direction of its body, so that the meat should be sliced lengthwise. In case the *ika* is so small that it has to be unavoidably sliced sidewise, always make sure to make cuts in the meat so as to cut the muscle fibers. For boiled *ika*, spread with *nitsume* (boiled down broth) to eat.

# *Tako* (Octopus)

Up until about 40 to 50 years ago, *tako* had been regarded as the lowest class of sushi-*dane*. *Tako* is called "devil fish" and is not considered edible in Europe and America. However, it is a fairly popular food in Japan, and nowadays, it is also a popular sushi-*dane*.

**Characteristics and Taste**    There are many varieties of *tako*, but only a few varieties are considered edible. It is *ma-dako* that is served by sushi shops in almost all cases. Undoubtedly, it is the tastiest of all edible varieties of *tako*.

*Tako* is basically the same as *ika* in its body construction. Eight legs have two rows of suckers each. It has pigment cells on the surface of the body, and can change its color according to its surroundings. When attacked by an enemy, it ejects a large amount of ink to hide itself in and flee. Fresh *tako* is generally grayish-white and has spots on its skin. The sucking disks are elastic and have a strong sucking force. The meat of *tako* consists of only about 15 percent protein with the rest being mostly water. The meat of *ma-dako* caught in the sea near Japan is especially tasty, and its meat is unparalleled in elasticity and firmness and its flavor is far superior than any of the other sea *ma-dako* varieties. The season is in January and February.

**How to Prepare**    As it is difficult to tell whether *tako* is fresh or not, it is necessary to pay special attention to the freshness of *tako* meat. In case of

raw *tako*, it is not fresh enough if its suckers are not elastic and if its body is sticky. In the case of boiled *tako*, it is rather easy to detect it when it is not fresh enough, as its skin comes off easily.

Today, *tako* is served as sushi-*dane* after being boiled in almost all cases. Wring it with salt well and wash it. Then put it in boiling water, and cool it in cold water. Boiled *tako* is offered on the market. Slice the leg meat on an angle into thin pieces from the thicker part. Originally, *tako* was served spread with *nitsume*. However, today sometimes it is served with *wasabi* (Japanese horseradish), without *nitsume*.

In former days, cooked *tako* was frequently used as sushi-*dane*. After washing the meat in water, pass it through boiling water for 4 to 5 seconds. Put a small amount of broth (made by adding a small amount of water and soy sauce to rice wine and then adding a small amount of sugar to the mixture) in a pan, and when it boils, put the legs that have been cut off in it, and boil them covered with a lid. Boil them for 30 to 40 minutes or one hour, and slice them just the same way as you would for boiled *tako*.

# *Torigai* (Cockle)　*Mirugai* (Horse-Neck Clam)
# *Akagai* (Red Clam)

# Hokkigai (Surf Clam)
# Awabi (Abalone)

## Shellfish as Sushi-*Dane*

Shellfish has been used for a long time as *nimono-dane* for *Edo*-style hand-formed sushi, as the Bay of Tokyo once abounded in shellfish. Today almost all shellfish are mainly used as raw *tane*, except for clams which need to be boiled. Because of its characteristic taste, shellfish serves as a kind of savory delicacy having the ability to kill the after-taste. In contrast to these tastes of heavy, light and oily fish meat, shellfish offers a fresh taste which is very soft to the palate. And the fact that it has to be chewed with some amount of force provides a feeling that no other sushi-*dane* can give.

# Torigai (Cockle)

Among the many types of shellfish used for sushi-*dane*, torigai is particular well known and popular for its good taste. Its resilient meat is very pleasing to the palate. Today, it is mainly served raw.

**Characteristics** *Torigai* is a bivalve-type shellfish about 4 inches (10 cm) in length. The outer shell is yellowish-white and the inner shell has a reddish-purple color. The long foot-like part is blackish-purple and slightly curved. This is the portion that is used as sushi-*dane*. In most cases, this portion is separated from the shell at the time they are taken from the sea, and is marketed after being boiled and opened. It spawns twice a year, in spring and autumn, and the season for this shellfish is from August to April. The thicker the meat, the more it is valued.

**How to Prepare** Use it after removing the entrails in thin salt water. It can be enjoyed as it is or after passing it through boiling water once and then washing it quickly in thinly sweetened vinegar. Handle it with special care and do not touch the top surface too much, or the beautiful blackish-purple color may be lost to some extent.

# Mirugai (Horse-Neck Clam)

This shellfish gets tasty about the time when abalone gets out of season. It is one of the most important shellfish as sushi-*dane*, using the siphon part of the shellfish mainly. It is a high class *tane* and is particularly pleasant on the teeth.

**Characteristics** *Mirugai*, also called *mirukuigai*, is a large-size bivalve, about 5 inches (12 cm) long and 4 inches (9 cm) high. The white surface of the shell is covered with a thick dark brown skin. It stretches a long and large siphon into the sea and at the end of which it is usually found a seaweed called "*miru*" (thick-haired codium), and from this it derived its name. It is available on the market all the year round, but the season is from February to June so that it follows that of *abalone*. The siphon is covered with a hard, black skin, and with thick meat, it is hard to masticate and very tasty. To see whether it is fresh or not, pull the siphon. If it is tough and does not yield easily, it is fresh.

**How to Prepare** Remove the meat from the shell, cut off the siphon part, wash it well in water, and then peel off the skin. Dip it quickly in boiling water, and soon cool it in cold water, which will allow the skin to be easily peeled away from the beak-shaped tip of the siphon. Open it by cutting the center part with a knife, and wash away any sand inside. And then, if desired, more color can be added to it. In order to make it more vivid and colorful, cut off the tip of the siphon, put only the end part of it in boiling water shaking it back and forth quickly. (This process is called "*yu-buri*", shaking in boiling water). Put it in cold water and drain off. In this way, the siphon becomes beautiful, pale crimson. Cut the siphon into pieces in such a way so as to take full advantage of the beautiful red color. Make lengthwise cuts in them so that the harder-to-digest meat can be easily eaten. The correct way of preparing *mirugai* is to wash them by lightly wringing out the water. In this way, an odor peculiar to *mirugai* will be removed giving them a fine taste.

The other parts of the shellfish such as the tongue, mantle lobes, adductor muscles, etc. can be used as *tane* for hand-formed sushi and also as *tane* for *mixed sushi*.

# Akagai (Red Clam, Ark Shell)

It has a beautiful, bright reddish-orange-colored meat. This clam is a bit tough, but it is just this toughness combined with its unique savory taste. This very popular sushi-*dane*, is often referred to as the "king of shellfish."

**Characteristics** *Akagai* is a medium-sized bivalve-type shellfish about 3 inches (8 cm) in length with the surface of its shell being blackish-brown in color. The English equivalent is "red clam", and true to its name, it is reddish-orange in color. The shellfish in the cold season is called "real" *akagai*, with the shell being more blackish and the meat much redder. Summertime *akagai* is called "white *akagai*," with its shell and meat being whitish in color. The real *akagai* is tastier, while most of white *akagai* has thinner meat and is watery. The season is from October to March. While its meat is tasty, its adductor muscles and mantle lobes are also true delicacies and are loved by real connoisseurs of sushi. Always make sure that *akagai* is fresh, for it is very poisonous if it is not fresh.

**How to Prepare** Remove the meat from the shell, and separate the meat from the mantle lobes. Make a cut into the center of clam and put your knife under the meaty portion of the clam driving it in to the point where the clam is almost cut into two. Clean away any of the viscous matter from the meaty part. Wash it in water and drain off. Various cuts are made in the meat and cuts are also made around its fringe to give it a more beautiful, appealing look. Formerly, it was used as sushi-*dane*

after being dipped in vineger quickly. Today, however, it is served as it is in most cases.

In case the mantle lobes are used as sushi-*dane*, cut and open the adductor muscles at the end of the mantle lobes as thin as the mantle lobes. Before using the mantle lobes, sprinkle salt on it and remove slimy matter from it.

# Hokkigai (Surf Clam)

*Hokkigai* is sushi-*dane* used widely in the Tohoku District and Hokkaido, nothern Japan. However, even in Tokyo, sushi shops compete with each other in getting some of it to serve to their customers when in season.

**Characteristics**    Its formal name is *ubagai*, but it is better known as *hokkigai* at sushi shops. It is a bivalve-type shellfish about 4 to 6 inches (10 to 15 cm) in length, with a thick and heavy shell. Its top surface is grayish-yellow and is covered with a thick brown layer of skin. The meat is a pale purplish-brown and the shell has two adductor muscles. The season is from winter to spring. With a sweetish flavor of its own, it is very tasty. It is valued not only as sushi-*dane* but also as *sashimi* and *sunomono* (vinegared dish). Its adductor muscles are also used as sushi-*dane*.
**How to Prepare**    As sushi-*dane*, it is served raw or after being dipped quickly in hot water. As raw

sushi-*dane*, it is blackish at the tip, but if it is dipped in hot water (*yu-buri*), the dipped part will turn a purplish crimson, giving it a beautiful, appealing look. As it is usually obtained after being removed from its shell, it is better to dip it once in hot water so as to prevent its staleness.

In case it is served raw, open it up as far as its purplish tip. In case it is dipped in hot water, open it halfway up the white part. In this way, the maximum effect of the color can be obtained.

When the adductor muscles are used as sushi-*dane*, the blackish part along the fringe should be cleaned with a cloth.

# Awabi (Abalone)

*Awabi* is an important high-class sushi-*dane* particularly in summer. Formerly, it was boiled in broth and sliced to be served with *nitsume*. Today, it is usually served raw.

**Characteristics**    *Awabi* is a kind of sea snail, the large ones growing to a size of about 8 inches (20 cm) in diameter. Several kinds of *awabi* are served as food, but the kinds of *awabi* used as sushi-*dane* are *kuro-awabi* (black abalone, also being called *ogai* and *aogai*) and *megai-awabi* (red abalone). *Kuro-awabi* has tough, bluish-black meat and is suitable for sushi-*dane* raw and *sashimi*. *Megai-awabi* has reddish, soft meat, and is suited to be steamed or boiled in a broth. There is another important kind of *awabi* called *madaka-awabi*, which has thick and soft brown meat, which is highly praised as a high-class sushi-*dane*.

*Awabi* is in season during the summer months in contrast to the fact that most other shellfish are in season from winter to spring. The meat of *awabi* has a pleasant feeling when chewed and is loved for its unique and refined sweetness.
**How to Prepare**    *Awabi* must only be served raw if it is still alive. You can make sure it is fresh by pricking it at which time it will contract showing

that it is still living.

*Awabi* is roundish on one side and a little pointed on the other side. Its mouth is on the pointed side. Open the mouth with a knife and put salt in it, striking the shell on the roundish side lightly to make sure the salt spreads all over the body. When the meat hardens up, remove the meat from the shell. Cut away any visceral matter and the mantle lobes, and wash the meat clean in water. Slice the meat on a slight angle and serve the sliced meat after beating it. The adductor muscles of *awabi* are large and tasty and can be used as sushi-*dane*.

In the event frozen *awabi* is used, first steam it quickly, then steam it again in a pressure cooker. In this way, the meat of *awabi* will become soft and easy to handle.

In case you use it as *nimono-dane* called *mushi-awabi*, boil it once in water and then boil it for a second time for a longer period of time in a broth, or steam it in salt and served it topped with *nitsume*. (See photo on page 59).

●*Mushi-Awabi* (Steamed Abalone)... See photo on page 59.

# *Aoyagi* (Skimmer) & *Kobashira* (Adductor of Skimmer)  *Tairagai* (Tairagi Shellfish)

# *Hamaguri* (Clam)

In former days, *hamaguri* was widely used as *nimono-dane* essential for *Edomae*-zushi. Today, it is not so widely used as it was in the past. *Hamaguri* is the king of the bivalve-type shellfish and has been loved by Japanese since ancient times.

**Characteristics** It lives in sandy, shallow waters near the mouths of rivers. The surface of the shell is colored with a variety of colors—whitish, brown, purplish-brown, etc. It is said that each *hamaguri* has its own pattern of the shell and its own tooth shape of the hinge plates. Its season is from October to March, and the taste deteriorates in the spawning season which is from May through August. The meat is strongly sweet, though it is a refined sweetness. Due to its heavy and yet unique flavor, it is loved by all connoisseurs of sushi. *Hamaguri* is never used raw, but is served as *nimono-dane*.

**How to Prepare** In most cases, sushi shops buy de-shelled *hamaguri*. It is necessary to choose fleshy meat with a firm visceral mass. There is something about fresh *hamaguri* meat that gives off a general feeling of freshness when eaten.

Insert a long chopstick or something similar into the syphons having two blackish mouths of several de-shelled *hamaguri* one after another, hold both ends of the stick and wash the de-shelled *hamaguri* by turning the stick several times in the water. After shaking off the water, boil them in the following way. Put an adequate amount of *hamaguri* in boiling water, and when the water begins to boil again, pour another glass of water into it. Repeat this and when the water boils for the third time,

the *hamaguri* are considered to be properly boiled. Scoop the *hamaguri* up quickly with a bamboo basket, and spread them out as widely as possible to let them cool naturally. Pinch the blackish entrails which can be seen through the transparent meat with your fingers, and if the entrails have an elastic feel to them, the *hamaguri* are considered to be properly boiled. When they have cooled, open them up with a knife from the side of the meat and remove the entrails.

Next proceed to the "*tsukekomi*" process. If you boil *hamaguri* the meat will become hard. Therefore, when cooking, the so-called "*tsukekomi*" method should be employed. Arrange pieces of *hamaguri* meat in a square bowl, and pour seasoning mixture on them, and leave them as they are for at least 3 to 4 hours. (Turn over the meat halfway through the process). The seasoning mixture is prepared by boiling down a mixture of 60 percent soy sauce and 40 percent *mirin* (sweet cooking rice wine) with a proper amount of sugar until it has a sticky texture to it.

In using *hamaguri* as sushi-*dane*, never fail to press *hamaguri* with a dishcloth to remove any surplus sauce, and to remove completely what remains of the entrails inside. Serve *hamaguri* covered with *nitsume*.

# *Hotategai* (Scallop)

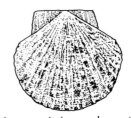

Its large adductor muscle is used as sushi-*dane*. At sushi shops in the districts where *hotategai* is caught, it is served raw. In Tokyo and other cities, it is usually served as *nimono-dane*. It is also served raw as *sashimi* and side dishes.

**Characteristics** *Hotategai* is a large-sized, round bivalve-type shellfish, with the large ones having a diameter of some 8 inches (20 cm). Of the two valves, one is white and bulges like the pan, while the other is purplish-brown in color being almost flat. It has no teeth like *hamaguri* in the hinge part, but the two valves are connected by a ligament. It has a large adductor muscle almost in the center, and it is this adductor muscle that is eaten. At present, almost all *hotategai* on the market are cultured ones. Its season is in winter. The meat is marked by a light, sweet taste.

**How to Prepare** Take out the meat from the shell, remove the black visceral mass, and separate the adductor muscle from the mantle lobes. Clean the adductor muscle and wash it in water. In case it is eaten raw, slice the adductor and use the sliced

meat as sushi-*dane*. In case it is used as *nimono-dane*, dip it in boiling water quickly and put it in a boiling seasoning mixture, and boil quickly. Take care not to boil it too much, as the meat becomes hard. The seasoning mixture is made by mixing 50 percent soy sauce with 50 percent water, with a proper amount of sugar added to the mixture. Rice wine and *mirin* (sweet rice wine) may also be added to vary the taste.

You may also boil the adductor muscle together with the visceral mass and the mantle lobes, and use them together as *nimono-dane*.

Slice the adductor muscle horizontally as sushi-*dane*, or crush it, and place the crushed part on the sushi. In the latter case, the sushi can be formed into a much better shape. Spread *nitsume* on it prior to serving.

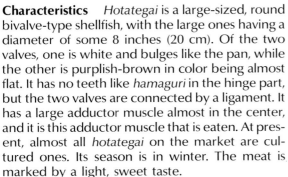

# *Anago* (Conger Eel)
# *Shako* (Mantis Shrimp)

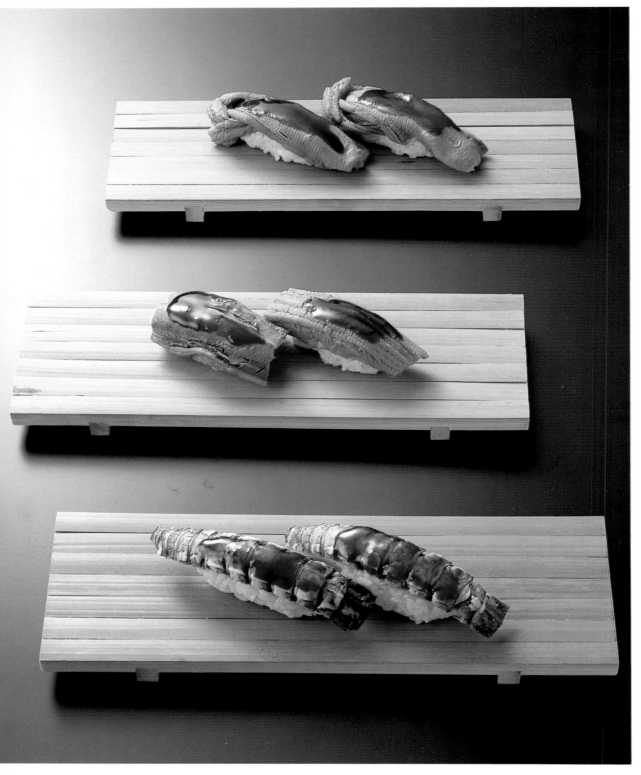

*Anago* (top and center), *Shako* (bottom)

# Komochi-Wakame (Seaweed with Herring Roe)
# Tobiuonoko (Flying-Fish Roe)　Ikura (Salmon Roe)
# Kazunoko (Herring Roe)　Uni (Sea Urchin)

## What Is Nimono-Dane?

What is called *nimono-dane* at sushi shops is the kind of *tane* that is served after boiled, spread with *nitsume* prepared by boiling down a mixture with special seasoning ingredients. Today, *anago, shako* and *tako* are about the only toppings that are used as *nimono-dane*. Formerly, *ika, awabi, hamaguri* and many others were also used as *nimono-dane*.

Nimono-dane has several advantages. It can utilize materials which are no longer fresh enough and also can be kept in stock longer. Also, sushi-dane becomes more digestible when served in this way. Further, *nimono-dane* is capable of removing or lessening the disagreeable smell or taste of the raw ingredients, thus making the sushi-dane more attractive.

## Other Sushi-Dane

Here, we will introduce several other sushi-*dane* which are not traditional ones but which have come to be used extensively in recent years. These are roe and ovaries of various kinds of fish. In addition to these, there is a tendency to use cod roe, smelt roe, pike conger roe, crab roe, shrimp roe, cuttlefish roe and other roe as sushi-*dane*. These roe *tane* are conveniently used by sushi shops in order to give variety to their menus.

Komochi-Wakame (upper left), Tobiuonoko (upper right), Ikura (center left), Kazunoko (center right), Uni (bottom)

# *Anago* (Conger Eel)

The cooking method of *anago* has long been studied and various techniques have been developed so that it is said that if one eats *anago* sushi, one can know the degree of the sushi-making skill of a sushi shop. *Anago* is a representative *nimono-dane*, and an essential *tane* for *Edomae* hand-formed sushi.

**Characteristics**  At a glance, *anago* looks like an eel (*unagi*). Being long and cylindrical, it does not have a ventral fin, but its dorsal, caudal and anal fins form one continuous fin. It takes 4 to 5 years to mature and is said to spawn once when it is about 10 years old.

Of the varieties of *anago*, that which is used as sushi-*dane* is ma-anago. Its body is pale-gray, and its back is glossy and grayish-brown, while the stomach side is a very bright white. There is a row of white spots on its both sides, which is lacking in other varieties of *anago*. Strictly speaking, the backs of some *anago* are blackish, while those of others are yellowish. The latter are more highly valued. Furthermore, fleshy *anago* is considered a high-class *tane*. A fully grown *anago* can reach a length of 3 feet (90 cm).

The taste of *anago* does not change very much throughout the year, and if there is a season for it, it is in summer when they are caught in relatively large quantities. The meat is not so oily and its taste is light. If *anago* is cooked with sugared broth, it is possible to draw out its characteristic taste. The real taste of hand-formed *anago* sushi is in the fact that the taste of *anago* matches the sourness of sushi rice.

**How to Prepare**  Every sushi shop has its own technique method for cooking *anago*, so that it may be said that there is no definitive way of cooking *anago*. However, I would like to present the method we used in cooking *anago* at my sushi shop.

First, fix an *anago* on the cooking board by driving a nail or some other pointed object through its head (*me-uchi*), and make a cut in the neck part with a knife, cutting it open from the back side. Then, wash *anago* in water, stirring it several times. Put *anago* in a bamboo basket to allow the water to drain off, and place it in another bamboo basket with the skin side upward, and stretch it well.

Next, prepare the seasoning mixture. Mix thick soy sauce, *mirin*, and water at a ratio of 1:2:1, and add a proper amount of sugar if necessary. Put the mixture in a pan, and boil it using a strong fire. When the mixture boils, put *anago* in with the skin side upward, and cover it, and when the mixture begins to boil again, lift the cover, and if they are entangled, unwind them. Place the cover on again, and boil *anago* using a medium fire for a long time. If about 20 *anago*, each about 8 to 10 inches (20 to 25 cm) in length are to be cooked at one time, boil them for about 15 to 20 minutes. When *anago* are cooked, turn off the fire, leaving *anago* as they are to steam for another 15 to 20 minutes, and then remove them from the pan. They are ready to be served after about 1 hour.

Cut *anago* into pieces properly according to its size. In the case of a medium-sized *anago*, cut it into two parts, that is, the upper half from the head, and the lower half on the tail side. The upper half is served with the skin side upward, and the lower half with the meat side upward.

In the case of larger one, slice it on an angle or cut it into thin slices. Form sushi softly, and top it with *nitsume*. In this case, no *wasabi* (Japanese horseradish) is used.

# *Shako* (Mantis Shrimp)

Until about 50 to 60 years ago, sushi shops had no interest in *shako*. Today, it is a well-established *nimono-dane*. A *shako*, with an ovary, called "katsubushi", is particularly tasty and is highly valued.

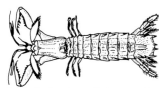

**Characteristics**  *Shako* is a grotesque-shaped crustacean, but its taste is like the taste of crab mingled with that of shrimp. The body color of raw *shako* is grayish-brown, but when boiled, its color becomes a pale reddish-purple. It is about 6 inches (15 cm) long. Its season is from May to June. *Shako* with roe is particularly tasty.

**How to Prepare**  As *shako* gets stale easily, it is boiled as soon as it is bought in the marketplace in the fishing ports, after which it is made available to sushi shops. Therefore, sushi shops only cut and serve it. High quality *shako* is palish purple and glossy, and the meat is firm and thick. Cut off the tip of the tail part, and press the meat lightly with the palm of your hand so as to flatten the skin side of the meat as much as possible before serving it. Serve it with *nitsume* or *wasabi* (Japanese horseradish).

It is interesting to note that up until 20 to 30 years ago, many sushi shops served *shako* after quickly boiling it in sugar.

# Komochi-wakame (Seaweed with Herring Roe)

Komochi-wakame is seaweed (wakame) on which herring has spawned, covering the seaweed with roe. Komochi-wakame being a new sushi-dane has a pleasant feeling to the palate when eaten and is highly praised for its taste. As it is salted, dip it in thinly salted water for about 2 hours to remove the salt. Use it as it is or wind a strip of nori around it.

Komochi-konbu is konbu (kelp) on which herring has spawned. Treat it in the same way as komochi-wakame.

# Tobiuonoko (Flying-Fish Roe)

Tobiuonoko being colorful and inviting is also a new sushi-dane. It is also called golden caviar. As sushi-dane, it is much lower in cost than ikura, and so it is used as a substitute for ikura. There are two varieties of tobiuonoko, that is, those which are reddish and those which are yellowish. It is served, in a gunkan-maki style.

# Ikura (Salmon Roe)

This is a relatively new sushi-dane, but it is now fully established one. Raw ikura is obtainable only in areas where the salmon are caught, so that usually it is salted ikura that is served by sushi shops. The ovaries are removed artificially from salmon just before the spawning season, with roe being separated one by one.

Roe that is bright red and glossy, full and having no wrinkles is high quality ikura. If it is exposed to air, it will become whitish in color, with its outside surface becoming hard and having wrinkles. In such a case, spray rice wine on it or soak it in rice wine, and it will be restored to its original state. It should be kept in a refrigerator.

There is no need to prepare ikura specially before it is served. Like sea urchin roe, ikura is served, in a gunkan-maki style.

# Kazunoko (Herring Roe)

Kazunoko is a new high-class sushi-dane that came to be used during the postwar period. Formerly, it was available in the form of dried kazunoko, but it came to be popular after salted kazunoko came to be available easily on the market.

As the number of roe in the ovary of a herring is so large, Kazunoko has long been regarded as a propitious food, symbolizing abundance. Kazunoko with eggs of the same size, thick and without cracks in it is considered good, while whitish kazunoko with small-size eggs, is not mature and poor in quality.

As almost only salted kazunoko is used, always remember to remove the salt from it. While soaking it in water thinly salted for 3 to 4 hours, clean away any membrane and scale. Change water several times. Drain off the water, and serve it as it is (sometimes with a strip of nori) or serve it, in a gunkan-maki style.

# Uni (Sea Urchin)

This is a representative sushi-dane that has rapidly become popular since the end of World War II. Uni roe is eaten raw, and when they are not fresh enough, they are served after being steamed.

Uni belongs to a class of oblate echinoderms, and is spherical or hemispherical in shape. It is enclosed in a hard shell covered with spines. Of the varieties of uni, those which are edible include bafun-uni, murasaki-uni, and ezo-bafun-uni. The part of uni that is eaten raw is the developed ovary, which is called nama-uni.

Fresh nama-uni is firm and smells good. It should be wrapped and kept in a refrigerator. If it is not fresh enough, it is soft and shapeless, as well as being watery.

Nama-uni is used as it is. In many cases, sushi rice is rolled in nori (toasted seaweed), and is topped with nama-uni, in a gunkan-maki style. (See photo on page 63).

## About Nitsume

Formerly, many different kinds of nitsume were prepared and used with nimono-dane. For example, hamaguri broth was boiled down to obtain nitsume for hamaguri nimono-dane. Today, one of the most popular nitsume is obtained by boiling down anago broth and is used for all kinds of nimono-dane.

Anago nitsume is made in the following way. Use anago broth which has already boiled anago several times (for how to boil anago, please refer to the section on anago), and filter it in cheesecloth. Add sugar, mirin and soy sauce to it, and boil it to remove any harshness. After boiling it once, allow it to boil down under low heat. During the summer months, boil it down to 30 percent of its volume, and in winter, to 40 percent.

Dip a chopstick into nitsume and if nitsume is thick enough to stick to it, having a stringy-like texture, then it is ready.

# Nori-Maki (Sushi Rolls)
# Tamago-Yaki (Omelet)

# Nori-Maki (Sushi Rolls with Toasted Seaweed)

*Edomae* sushi roll means a sushi roll with toasted seaweed. The three representative types of *Edomae* sushi rolls are *tekka-maki* (with tuna inside), *kappa-maki* (with cucumber), and *kampyo-maki* (with seasoned gourd strips).

*Edomae* sushi rolls have a long history. They started as an important kind of sushi together with the beginning of *Edomae* sushi. In those days, large quantities of high quality seaweed (*Asakusa-nori*) were obtained from the Bay of Tokyo, and "*Asakusa-nori* sushi rolls" were very popular then. Its flavor and pleasing touch to the palate matched well the sushi rice and the various ingredients rolled in it to produce a special taste. It was used, so to speak, as a side dish for raw fish or *nimono-dane* sushi.

According to size and shape, sushi rolls are classed into "*hoso-maki*" (thin rolls), "*futo-maki*" (also called ō-*maki*, thick rolls), "*no-no-ji-maki*" (rolls whose cross-section shows the pattern of the Japanese *Kana* letter "の=no", or *no-no-ji*), etc. The most important of these for *Edomae* sushi rolls is the *hoso-maki* sushi roll.

Sushi rolls are called differently according to "*gu*" (ingredients contained in them). However, there are some kinds of sushi rolls with special names such as *tekka-maki* and *kappa-maki*.

Today, we have a large variety of sushi rolls, including hand-rolled sushi, and many different "*gu*" are used for *nori-maki*. These have contributed greatly toward enriching the menus of sushi shops.

Toasted seaweed is always used for *Edomae* sushi rolls, and its crispness is highly valued. By the way, untoasted seaweed is always used for Kansai sushi rolls. *Nori-maki* with softened toasted seaweed lose much of its value. Therefore, *nori-maki* should be made and served quickly.

**Hoso-Maki and Futo-Maki**    A sheet of toasted seaweed is cut into two and a half of it is used with "*gu*" as the core to make a *hoso-maki*, whereas a full sheet of toasted seaweed is used to make a *futo-maki*. A large variety of "*gu*" are used for *nori-maki*—seasoned gourd strips, tuna, cucumber, *oboro* (whitefish flakes), omelet, mushroom, etc. In the case of *hoso-maki*, a sheet of toasted seaweed is usually cut in half sideways. A half cut sideways is slightly larger in width than a half cut lengthwise so that it is easier to handle the former in making a sushi roll.

Almost all *hoso-maki* are traditionally wound in a round cross-section, while some are wound in a square cross-section.

**How to Cut Nori-Maki**    A *nori-maki* is cut into pieces to be served. The cut pieces have varying tastes according to their size, even if the materials are the same. It is necessary to adjust the size according to different kinds of "*gu*".

Formerly, a *hoso-maki* was cut into two, and then later into three. In the postwar period, it came to be cut into four pieces in almost all cases with a few exceptions. This is very convenient for sushi shops. If a sushi roll is cut into four pieces, these four can be served to two persons, two each. However, a *hoso-maki* with seasoned gourd strips tastes best when cut into three, and you can relish the real taste of *tekka-maki* when a roll is cut into six pieces.

● *Kampyo-Maki* (With Seasoned Gourd Strips)
The *kampyo-maki* is a traditional sushi roll, which uses seasoned gourd strips as the core. As it looks like a gun barrel, it is also called "*teppo-maki*" (gun roll). It is rolled round and is cut into three pieces for serving. Recently, many sushi shops cut into four pieces.

Here is how to make a sushi roll. Use the "*maki-su*" (the rolling mat; a small-size bamboo screen for making sushi rolls), and spread the longer side of a *nori-sheet* half along the edge, close to you, of the *maki-su*. Put a quantity of sushi rice enough for three pieces of hand-formed sushi on the left side of the center of the *maki-su*, and spread the rice in all directions, and make the center of the sushi rice thin to place seasoned gourd strips there. Do not use *wasabi*(Japanese horseradish) in this case. Lift the *maki-su* on the near side of you. Then, roll the *maki-su* to the edge of sushi rice and press the roll firmly. Remove the *maki-su* and shape the sushi roll by pressing it from both sides.

● *Tekka-maki* (With Tuna)
*Tekka-maki* is a sushi roll with tuna, which made its debut toward the end of the *Edo* period (in the middle of 19th C.). It is one of the most important of *Edomae* sushi rolls. Leftover tuna meat produced at the time of "*sakudori*" (see photos on page 33) is used as the core for *tekka-maki*. The tuna meat should be cut somewhat shorter than the width of the toasted seaweed.

*Tekka-maki* is rolled in about the same way as *kampyo-maki*.

Usually, a *tekka-maki* is cut into six pieces, which are served with the core upward.

● *Kappa-Maki* (With Cucumber)
This is a relatively new sushi roll with toasted seaweed, which uses cucumber as the core, representing a delightful combination of *Edomae* sushi roll and vegetable.

Use a cucumber after passing it through boiling water and cooling it in cold water so as to make it much more colorful. Make a *kappa-maki* and cut it in just the same way as the *tekka-maki*.

# Tamago-Yaki (Omelet)

In former days, every sushi shop served its own homemade *tamago-yaki*. Making *tamago-yaki* was one of the most important tasks for *Edomae*-zushi shops, like preparing shining *tane* and *nimono-dane*. It was said in the past that how a sushi shop prepared *tamago-yaki* showed the particular skill of that shop. Surely, the seasoning of *tamago-yaki* is extremely difficult and complex, and baking it is equally demanding. Because of this, the preparation and use of *tamago-yaki* allow the sushi maker to create it demonstrating the individuality and skill of their sushi shop.

Today, *tamago-yaki* offered at sushi shops is ready-made and can be purchased mostly anywhere fish or fish-related foods are sold, so that it has lost much of the meaning it once possessed. However, there is a possibility of this being re-evaluated by sushi shops since more and more sushi shops are compelled to demonstrate their individuality and variety.

*Tamago-yaki* used by sushi shops can be classified into four kinds—*atsu-yaki* (thick-baked) and *usu-yaki* (wafer-thin-baked) *tamago* in which mashed fish meat is contained, and *dashi-maki* and *usu-yaki tamago* which does not contain mashed fish meat. The *tamago-yaki* available today on the market resembles *atsu-yaki tamago* and is close to the popular one which was made formerly by sushi shops. Here we will introduce one variety of *usu-yaki tamago* and its *kashiwa-zuke* that are made at our shop, as well as *dashi-maki tamago* which is now the leading type of *tamago-yaki* made by sushi shops.

## ●*Usu-Yaki Tamago* (Without Mashed Fish Meat)

Instead of mashed fish meat, use *komi* (shrimp and white-meat fish are boiled and minced), add small amounts of sugar, *mirin* (sweet rice wine), soy sauce and water, break the eggs over it and mix well. The addition of a small amount of water is a special seasoning method we use at my shop. Fry the mixture to a thickness of ⅕ inch (0.5 cm). In this case, use a pan shallower than the pan used for frying *atsu-yaki tamago*. Fry it while turning it over with a pair of chopsticks. It is very difficult to fry *usu-yaki-tamago* well. It is regarded as one of the tasks of sushi shops that requires the highest of skills.

After being cooked, cut it into pieces, placing one piece on each sushi. Or, according to the *kashiwa-zuke* style, cover sushi rice with a piece of *tamago-yaki* just as you would when making a *kashiwa-mochi*, which is Japanese traditional rice cake covered with an oak leaf. On the right in the picture (page 66) are shown the two *kashiwa-zuke* style sushi, one with three-cut pattern through which *oboro* is visible.

## ●*Dashi-Maki Tamago*

This is *tamago-yaki* made mainly in the kansai District. Different sushi shops use different kinds and quantities of seasonings. The following is just one example of how *dashi-maki tamago* is prepared. Put 8 eggs, ⅓ cup *dashi* (broth), 4 ounces (100 g) sugar, 1 tablespoon *mirin*, 2 tablespoons light soy sauce, and a pinch of salt in a bowl, and mix them well with the whisk. Then, put a Japanese omelet pan on medium heat, and oil it evenly and put half a ladle of the mixture in it. Spread the mixture evenly and when it is properly heated, fold it toward you in three layers. Oil the pan on the far side, and then push the folded mixture to that side, and oil the near side of the pan. Pour a ladle of the uncooked mixture into the pan, and spread it evenly also under the cooked mixture. When it is heated, fold them as a whole toward you in three layers. Repeat this process two more times until the cooked mixture becomes as thick as the depth of the pan. Move the cooked mixture to a block and shape it. Serve it after it has cooled without using *wasabi* (Japanese horseradish). You may band a *tamago-yaki* and sushi rice with a strip of toasted seaweed.

# The Pleasure of Sushi-Making

If you can make sushi yourself, the joy of eating sushi will be all the great-
er. However, it is rather difficult to make sushi. Now, of all the kinds of
sushi, we will show you how to make several kinds of sushi which are not
only very tasty but relatively easy to make.

# How to Cook Basic Sushi Ingredients

Pleasure is found not just in savoring sushi but also in making it. Of course, everything does not go the same way as in sushi bars (shops), but there are many types of sushi which can be made at home. Sushi we are going to introduce to you from page 74 are all fun to make at home and good to eat. Here, you will be shown how to prepare sushi ingredients used in many types of sushi.

## Sushi Rice

**Ingredients**
**(yields about 3 pounds = 1.4 kg)**
4 cups uncooked short-grained rice
4½ cups water
4-inch (10-cm) piece *konbu* (dried kelp)
Mix vinegar into rice after being cooked to season
    ½ cup rice vinegar
    2½ tablespoons sugar
    2⅓ teaspoons salt

**1.** Rince rice in water. Continuously stir rice, replacing water when it becomes cloudy, until water is almost clear.
**2.** Wipe *konbu* lightly with damp cloth to remove sand. Combine rinsed rice, water and *konbu* in a deep pot with a heavy bottom and tight-fitting lid (if you do not have a rice cooker) and let sit for 30 minutes.
**3.** Cover the pot and place it over a high fire. Bring to a boil and after 1 minute reduce heat to low and cook for 18 minutes. Turn the heat off and let steam for 10 minutes.
**4.** Put the ingredients for vinegar mixture in a saucepan and heat (do not boil) over a low fire, stirring until salt dissolves completely.
**5.** Remove *konbu* from cooked rice. Mix vinegar with rice well, using a spatula. Transfer to a bowl and let cool to body temperature.

## *Dashi* (Bonito Fish Stock)

**Ingredients (yields about 4 cups)**
4¼ cups water
4-inch (10-cm) piece *konbu* (dried kelp)
1 cup (⅕ ounce = 5 g) *katsuobushi* (dried bonito fish flakes)

**1.** Wipe *konbu* lightly with a damp cloth and cut into 4 pieces with scissors.
**2.** Put 4 cups of water and *konbu* into a pan and bring to a boil over a medium fire. Immediately after water begins to boil, remove *konbu*. Add ¼ cup of water to stop boiling.
**3.** Add *katsuobushi* all at one time. When water begins to boil again, turn off the heat. Strain *dashi* through a cheesecloth-lined sieve or an ordinary fine sieve.
**Note:** Instant soup stocks such as *katsuo-dashi* (a liquid bonito extract) and *konbu-dashi* (a liquid kelp extract) may be used. However, for the best possible taste, it is advisable to make your own bonito fish stock.

## Seasoned Mushrooms

**Ingredients**
10 dried mushrooms (*shiitake*)
3 tablespoons sugar
2 tablespoons soy sauce

**1.** Wash mushrooms. Reconstitute by soaking in ample amount of lukewarm water for 1 to 2 hours.

Wash dried mushrooms. Soak in lukewarm water for 1 to 2 hours and reconstitute. Remove stems.

Pour in enough liquid used to reconstitute until mushrooms are completely covered.

(Add water if there is not enough liquid.) Cover saucepan and simmer for 5 minutes. Add the other ingredients and continue to simmer until most of the liquid is gone.

**2.** Remove stems and place mushrooms in a saucepan. Pour in just enough of the soaking liquid to cover. Simmer for 5 minutes over low heat. Add sugar and soy sauce. Continue to simmer until most of the liquid is gone.

# Pickled Lotus Roots

**Ingredients**
4 ounces (100 g) lotus roots
1½ tablespoons rice vinegar
1½ tablespoons sugar
⅓ teaspoon salt
Rice vinegar for boiling water

**1.** Cut out V-shaped wedges between the holes lengthwise on the outside of lotus roots. Pare and slice thinly. Soak in lightly vinegared water to retain whiteness and eliminate harshness.
**2.** Add 1 tablespoon of vinegar to boiling water, put in lotus roots and blanch.
**3.** Bring vinegar, sugar and salt to a boil, add lotus roots and simmer over medium heat for 1 to 2 minutes.

Cut out V-shaped wedges between the holes. Pare, rounding the edges.

# *Oboro* (Whitefish Flakes)

**Ingredients**
6 ounces (150 g) white meat fish
3 tablespoons sugar
⅓ teaspoon salt
Small amount of red food coloring in powdered form (*shokubeni*)

**1.** Cook fish in boiling water for 8 minutes. Remove and discard skin, bones and guts. Wrap fish in cheesecloth (or dishcloth), knead vigorously under running water and wring dry. Open cloth and shred fish with fingers.
**2.** Place shredded fish in the top of a double boiler along with salt and dissolved food coloring. Put the pan in its bottom section and stir constantly with 4 to 5 wooden chopsticks or a fork. Add a little of sugar 3 to 4 times while stirring, and cook until the mixture puffs and swells like cotton.

Boil white meat fish for 8 minutes and drain. Remove all skin, bones, guts and dark meat.

Wrap in cheesecloth (or dishcloth). Knead vigorously under running water and wring out. Open cloth and shred meat with fingers.

Place shredded meat, salt and dissolved food coloring in a small double boiler. Stir and cook until the meat puffs and becomes fluffy. Meanwhile, add sugar a little bit 3 to 4 times.

**Ingredients**
(yields about 7 ounces, 200 g)
1 ounce (25 g) dried gourd strips
2 cups *dashi*
3 tablespoons sugar
2 tablespoons *mirin* (sweet rice wine for cooking)
2 tablespoons soy sauce

# Seasoned Gourd Strips (*Kampyo*)

**1.** Wash gourd strips in cold water. Rub with salt and wash again. Place in a saucepan, cover with water and let sit for a few minutes. Bring to a boil and simmer for about 10 minutes.
**2.** Drain well. Add *dashi*, sugar, *mirin* and soy sauce, and bring to a boil. When the mixture boils, reduce heat, cover and simmer for 30

minutes. When most of the liquid is gone, turn off the heat and let sit until cool.

Rub gourd strips with salt. Wash and let sit in water for a few minutes. Simmer for 10 minutes. Drain. With *dashi* and the other ingredients, cover and simmer over low heat until most of the liquid is gone.

# Seasoned Carrots

**Ingredients**
4 ounces (100 g) carrot
⅓ cup *dashi*
2 teaspoons sugar
A pinch of salt

**1.** Peel and cut carrot into the desired shape. Depending on the use, either julienne or cut into thin or slightly thicker rectangular pieces. (See recipes).
**2.** Put *dashi*, sugar, salt and carrots into a saucepan and simmer over low heat until tender or most of the liquid is gone.

# Wafer-Thin Omelets

**Ingredients (yields 12 in a frying pan, 6 inches by 6 inches (15 cm by 15 cm))**
10 eggs
3 tablespoons sugar
1 teaspoon salt
1 tablespoon potato starch or corn starch
3 tablespoons rice wine
Vegetable oil (as needed)

**1.** Beat eggs lightly. Strain into a bowl either through a wide-mesh strainer or put damp cheesecloth over the bowl and pour half of beaten egg into it. Strain it through cheesecloth, by continuously twisting it, forcing egg through the cloth. Repeat the process for the remainder of eggs.
**2.** Combine sugar, salt, starch and rice wine and mix well. Add the mixture to egg, and mix.
**3.** Liberally oil an omelet or a frying pan and heat over low heat. Pour off any excess oil and wipe to ensure evenness. Pour in about a half-ladle of the egg mixture, returning any excess to the bowl. Cook over low heat, taking care not to burn. When the surface looks slightly dry, run a pair of chopsticks or a fork under the omelet, lift and flip over. Cook the other side briefly, placing the finished omelet on a plate. Repeat the process for the remaining omelets.

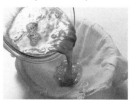  

Beat eggs lightly. Put damp cheesecloth over the bowl. Pour in half of beaten eggs.

Bring the 4 corners together and holding tightly, twist and force egg through the cloth. Combine potato starch and the other ingredients, and mix well.

Oil a frying pan over low heat. Pour in about a half-ladle of the egg mixture. When the surface looks dry, lift with the chopsticks or a fork and flip it over.

# Thick Omelet

**1.** Pound fish meat into small pieces. Purée it in a food processor or blender. Add *dashi*, sugar, *mirin*, starch and salt. Mix in lightly beaten egg a little at a time and stir well.
**2.** Liberally oil a 6-inch-by-6-inch (15-cm-by-15-cm) frying pan and heat, spreading oil evenly. Drain off any excess oil and place the pan over medium heat. Pour in egg mixture all at once. When the edges

## Ingredients (yields one)

4 eggs
1½ ounces (40 g) raw fish, white meat of cod, flounder or the like
2 tablespoons *dashi*
2 tablespoons sugar
1 tablespoon *mirin* (sweet rice wine for cooking)
1 tablespoon potato starch or cornstarch
⅓ teaspoon salt
Vegetable oil (as needed)

start to firm up, reduce the heat to low, cover and cook for about 5 minutes.

**3.** With the lid on, invert the pan and allow egg to fall onto the lid. Carefully shake egg back into the pan and cook the other side for a few seconds.

When edges firm up, reduce the heat. Cover and cook for about 5 minutes. With the lid on, invert the pan and allow egg to fall onto the lid. Carefully shake egg back into the pan and cook the other side.

## Ingredients

4 ounces (100 g) burdock
⅔ cup *dashi*
2 tablespoons rice wine
1 tablespoon sugar
2 teaspoons light-colored soy sauce
**Note:** Light-colored soy sauce gives a beautiful finish. If you do not have it, regular soy sauce may be used.

# Seasoned Burdock Shavings

**1.** Scrape off skin of the burdock with the backside of a knife. Score burdock with the knife by making long vertical slits on the sides at evenly space points. Whittle it as if sharpening a pencil. Soak for 10 minutes or so in water to prevent discoloring.

**2.** Drain off the shavings and put into a sauce pan. Add *dashi* and rice wine and cook for 5 minutes. Add sugar and soy sauce, and simmer over low heat until the liquid is almost gone.

Scrape off the skin of the burdock. Make 2 or 3 long vertical slits, and whittle it as if sharpening a pencil.

**See photo on page 79**

**4 Servings**
**Cooking time: 30 minutes**

2 pounds (900 g) sushi rice
4 ounces (100 g) carrots, seasoned
8 mushrooms, seasoned
12 sheets *shiraita-konbu* (a dried white kelp sheet)
    3 tablespoons sugar
    ½ cup rice vinegar
    ½ teaspoon salt
    1⅓ cups water
2 ounces (50 g) *mitsuba* (trefoil)

# *Konbu-Maki* (Sushi Rolled in *Konbu*)

Here, we can enjoy a taste different from other thick sushi rolled in *nori*.

| Calories 489 | Protein 8.1 g | Fats 2.1 g | Carbohydrates 109 g |
|---|---|---|---|

**1.** See "How to Cook Basic Sushi Ingredients" on pages 70 to 72 and prepare sushi rice, seasoned carrots and seasoned mushrooms.

**2.** Combine sugar, vinegar, salt and water in a saucepan. Add *konbu* and simmer for about 5 minutes, then let cool in the pan.

**3.** Cut carrots into match-stick size pieces. Slice mushrooms ⅕ inch (0.5 cm) thick. Blanch *mitsuba* for a few seconds and immerse into ice water to cool, and drain.

**4.** Lay 3 lengths of *konbu* across the rolling mat horizontally, starting a little up from the bottom of the mat. Let each strip overlap the one above by a fraction of 1 inch (2.5 cm). Spread ¼ of sushi rice over *konbu*, leaving a blank strip of about 1 inch (2.5 cm) at the top. Lay ¼ of carrots, mushrooms and *mitsuba* across the rice at the center in one line. Lift the end of the mat closest to you, roll almost one complete turn, stopping to press firmly, and then finishing the roll. Slice the roll into equal portions 1 inch (2.5 cm) thick. Repeat the process for the remaining 3 rolls.

73

# *Gomoku-Chirashi-Zushi* (Mixed Sushi)
# *Sake-Chirashi-Zushi* (Mixed Sushi Using Smoked Salmon)
# *Mushi-Zushi* (Steamed Sushi)

# Te-Maki-Zushi (Hand-Rolled Sushi)

**4 Servings**
**Cooking time: 1 hour**

3 pounds (1.4 kg) sushi rice
3 ounces (75 g) gourd strips, seasoned
4 mushrooms, seasoned
2 ounces (50 g) carrots, seasoned
2 ounces (50 g) pickled lotus roots
2 to 3 tablespoons *oboro* (whitefish flakes)
3 wafer-thin omelets
1 sheet *yaki-nori* (toasted seaweed)
12 snow peas
8 medium-size shrimps
  rice vinegar for boiling water
  2 teaspoons rice vinegar
  2 teaspoons sugar
  A pinch of salt

# *Gomoku-Chirashi*-Zushi
## (Mixed Sushi)

This is a popular homemade sushi. It uses colorful ingredients and has a good nutritional balance.

| Calories 517 | Protein 17.3 g | Fats 5.8 g | Carbohydrates 98.9 g |
|---|---|---|---|

**1.** See "How to Cook Basic Sushi Ingredients" on pages 70 to 73 and prepare sushi rice, seasoned gourd strips, seasoned mushrooms, seasoned carrots, pickled lotus roots, *oboro* and omelets.
**2.** Chop up gourd strips, mushrooms and carrots.
**3.** Minutely slice omelets so the strips look like shredded "golden threads". Place *nori* in a plastic bag and crumple it.
**4.** Remove all stems and stringy parts from all snow peas. Boil for about 2 minutes or until tender in lightly salted boiling water. Put directly into ice water. Drain and then cut a V-shape in the ends.
**5.** Devein shrimps and boil for 2 to 3 minutes in boiling water spiced lightly with vinegar. When cool, peel everything but tail section. Sprinkle with vinegar and sugar and set aside.
**6.** Lightly mix gourd strips, mushrooms and carrots into sushi rice. Transfer to a serving dish. Sprinkle the mixture with crumpled *nori*. Garnish with thinly sliced omelets, lotus roots, *oboro*, snow peas and shrimps.

**6 Servings**
**Cooking time: 45 minutes**

3 pounds (1.4 kg) sushi rice
7 ounces (175 g) smoked salmon
1 lemon
2 slender cucumbers
  ½ teaspoon salt
¾ ounce (20 g) fresh ginger
4 tablespoons white sesame seeds (toasted)

# *Sake-Chirashi*-Zushi
## (Mixed Sushi Using Smoked Salmon)

To use smoked salmon in sushi is a wonderful idea. Both the flavor and the sourness of lemon are a definite must.

| Calories 500 | Protein 19.5 g | Fats 6.5 g | Carbohydrates 90.9 g |
|---|---|---|---|

**1.** See "How to Cook Basic Sushi Ingredients" on page 70 and prepare sushi rice.
**2.** Slice smoked salmon thinly into bite-sized pieces. Quarter a lemon lengthwise, and squeeze ¼ lemon and sprinkle lemon juice over it and set aside.
**3.** Slice thinly each quarter crosswise (*ichogiri*) of the remaining lemon. Slice cucumbers thinly from the end, remove the seeds if they are hard. Salt, leaving for about 10 minutes until tender. Squeeze to remove any excess water.
**4.** Peel ginger and julienne finely. Soak in water for a few minutes and then squeeze to remove any excess water.
**5.** Mix smoked salmon, lemon, cucumbers, ginger and white sesame seeds into sushi rice.

# *Mushi*-Zushi (Steamed Sushi)

Sushi is normally not served warm, but this one is served hot. A microwave oven can be used instead of a steamer.

| Calories 514 | Protein 18.7 g | Fats 8.9 g | Carbohydrates 89.8 g |
|---|---|---|---|

**1.** See "How to Cook Basic Sushi Ingredients" on pages 70 to 72 and prepare sushi rice, seasoned mushrooms and seasoned carrots.

**4 Servings**
**Cooking time: 45 minutes**

1¾ pound (800 g) sushi rice
4 mushrooms, seasoned
4 ounces (100 g) carrots, cut into
  shape of match sticks and
  seasoned
6 ounces (150 g) chicken breasts
    1 tablespoon soy sauce
    1 tablespoon sugar
    2 tablespoons rice wine
2 eggs
    1 tablespoon sugar
    A pinch of salt
    1 tablespoon rice wine
½ cup green peas
    ½ teaspoon salt

**4 Servings**
**Cooking time: 1 hour, plus
  preparation time for fillets**

2 pounds (900 g) sushi rice
3 ounces (75 g) gourd strips,
  seasoned
½ thick omelet
4 horse mackerels
4 medium-size shrimps
½ whole squid
1 octopus tentacle, boiled
1 horse clam
1 block (6 ounces = 150 g) raw
  tuna
½ slender cucumber, de-seeded
½ avocado
1 pack *kaiware-na* (sprouts of long
  white radish)
8 green *shiso* leaves (beefsteak
  plant)
2 ounces (50 g) white *tosaka-nori*
  (one variety of seaweed),
  soaked in water to extract salt
4 fresh ginger stalks, pickled
8 sheets *yaki-nori* (toasted
  seaweed)
Small amount of salt, rice vinegar,
  sugar, lemon juice, powdered
  or freshly grated *wasabi*
  (Japanese green horseradish)

**2.** Slice chicken breasts and place in a pan. Add soy sauce, sugar and rice wine. Simmer until liquid is gone, turning sliced chicken over now and then.
**3.** Put eggs into a small saucepan and beat lightly. Mix in sugar, salt and rice wine. Using 4 to 5 chopsticks or a fork, stir over low heat to make scrambled eggs.
**4.** Put peas in a pan with 1 cup of water, add ½ teaspoon of salt, and boil until tender. Put in ice water to cool and then drain.
**5.** Put sushi rice into a deep container. Top with chicken, mushrooms, scrambled eggs, carrots and green peas. Place container in a steamer and steam over high heat for 10 to 15 minutes. If a microwave oven is used, allow for about 2 minutes per 1 serving. Serve hot.

# *Te-Maki*-Zushi (Hand-Rolled Sushi)

This is a kind of sushi which can be enjoyed easily at home. As for sushi-*dane*, you can combine others according to your own preference in addition to or instead of those we have introduced here.

| Calories 639 | Protein 44.2 g | Fats 11.8 g | Carbohydrates 102.5 g |

**1.** See "How to Cook Basic Sushi Ingredients" on pages 70 to 73 and prepare sushi rice, seasoned gourd strips and thick omelet.
**2.** Fillet each horse mackerel on both sides. Remove and discard any small bones around the abdominal cavity from the filleted halves. Throw all bony parts away. Sprinkle generously with salt and let sit for 30 minutes. Rinse off salt with vinegar. Remove the skin and any remaining small bones. Soak for 20 to 30 minutes in just enough vinegar to fully cover it. Make decorative slits in the outer surface of each filleted portion.
**3.** Devein shrimps. Skewer through the abdomen up to the tail. Boil in lightly salted and vinegared water for 2 minutes. Drain and then let cool. Remove the skewer by rotating and shell. Sprinkle on a bit of vinegar, sugar and salt and set aside.
**4.** Pull off the outer skin of squid, blanch and then immerse in ice water. Drain, pat dry and cut into thin slices. Make the same-size slices for octopus.
**5.** Briefly blanch the siphon of horse clam by passing it through boiling water for a few seconds. Skin and slice.
**6.** Cut tuna, cucumber, omelet and gourd into strips so that the length does not exceed half the width of *nori*. Halve, de-seed and peel avocado. Cut slices ½ inch (1 cm) thick, sprinkle on a little lemon juice and set aside.
**7.** Quarter each sheet of *yaki-nori*.
**8.** Put sushi rice on one plate and the other ingredients on another. Set out *yaki-nori*, *wasabi* and soy sauce separately.
**9.** To eat, spread a small amount of sushi rice onto ¼ sheet of *yaki-nori*. Lightly spread a very fine layer of *wasabi* over the rice, then put on any of the prepared ingredients that suits your taste, rolling the filling *nori* into the shape of a cone. Dip in soy sauce before eating. Another excellent way is to make it into the shape of a sandwich by folding the filling *nori* like a single slice of bread.

# Hoso-Maki-Zushi (Thin Sushi Rolls)
# Hana-Maki-Zushi (Sushi in Wisteria-Like Clusters)

# *Futo-Maki-Zushi* (Thick Sushi Rolls)
# *Ura-Maki-Zushi* (Inside-Out Rolls)
# *Konbu-Maki* (Sushi Rolled in *Konbu*)

Lining with this end of the rolling mat, place *nori* vertically. Spread sushi rice evenly leaving 1-inch (2.5-cm) blank across the top of the *nori*. Lay the omelet and vegetables a little this side of the center horizontally.

Holding the omelet and vegetables in place with your fingers, start raising the rolling mat from this side. Take this end all the way to the top of spreaded sushi rice and press down. Roll in the shape of a cylinder, pressing from the outside.

Roll the ingredients with the rolling mat, lightly a quarter turn to the other side, and press again. When rolling is completed, release the rolling mat, keeping the edges even.

**4 Servings**
**Cooking time: 30 minutes**

2 pounds (900 g) sushi rice
4 ounces (100 g) gourd strips, seasoned
1 block (4 ounces = 100 g) raw tuna
1 slender cucumber
6 sheets *yaki-nori* (toasted seaweed)
Small amount of powdered or freshly grated *wasabi* (Japanese green horseradish)
Rice vinegar for wetting fingers and dampening the knife
* This vinegar called "*te-zu*" is made from 4 tablespoons rice vinegar mixed in 1 tablespoons water, and once bring to a boil.

**4 Servings**
**Cooking time: 30 minutes**

2 pounds (900 g) sushi rice
½ cup *oboro* (whitefish flakes)
2 eggs
    1 tablespoon sugar
    A pinch of salt
    1 tablespoon rice wine
12 snow peas
9 sheets *yaki-nori* (toasted seaweed)
Small amount of salt
Rice vinegar for wetting fingers and dampening the knife

Line up 5 to 6 rolls with a little overlapping. Cut each roll into 8 equal parts.

# *Hoso-Maki-Zushi* (Thin Sushi Rolls)

These three sushi rolls are the most typical of all sushi rolls.

| Calories 485 | Protein 15.1 g | Fats 1.8 g | Carbohydrates 102.1 g |
|---|---|---|---|

**1.** See "How to Cook Basic Sushi Ingredients" on pages 70 to 72 and prepare sushi rice and seasoned gourd strips.
**2.** Slice tuna into four strips, making sure the length is less than the width of *nori*.
**3.** Cut gourd strips into lengths that match the width of *nori*.
**4.** Cut cucumber lengthwise into 4 strips and de-seed.
**5.** Cut *nori* in half lengthwise. Place one half on the rolling mat. Wet your fingers and palms with rice vinegar and put about one twelfth (¹⁄₁₂) of sushi rice on *nori*, spreading it evenly and flat, and leaving a blank strip at the top of *nori* about ½ inch (1 cm) deep. Smear a line of *wasabi* evenly across the rice a little below the center. Place a slice of tuna on the line. Lift the end of the mat closest to you, and press down on the rolling mat to stabilize. Roll the mat almost one complete turn, making sure it does not become part of the roll and that *nori* goes under the rice. Roll in the shape of a cylinder.
**6.** Repeat the process for gourd strips and cucumber, but in the former case avoid using *wasabi*.
**7.** Cut each roll into 4 or 6 equal slices, dampening the cutting knife between each slice by running it across a cloth that has been dampened with rice vinegar. Dip the slices in soy sauce to eat. Garnish with *kaiware-na* and sweat-and-sour ginger, if desired.

# *Hana-Maki-Zushi*
# (Sushi in Wisteria-Like Clusters)

A cute, little sushi in the shape of a flowery cluster. This type is rolled thinner than regular sushi rolls.

| Calories 496 | Protein 11.5 g | Fats 4.2 g | Carbohydrates 103.1 g |
|---|---|---|---|

**1.** See "How to Cook Basic Sushi Ingredients" on pages 70 to 71 and prepare sushi rice and *oboro*.
**2.** Beat eggs lightly in a small saucepan. Mix in sugar, salt and rice wine. Over low heat, stir with 4 to 5 chopsticks or a fork to make finely scrambled egg.
**3.** Remove all stems from snow peas. Boil for about 2 minutes or until tender in lightly salted boiling water. Put directly into ice water to cool and then drain. Cut into needle-thin pieces. Sprinkle with a small amount of salt and set aside.
**4.** Divide sushi rice into 3 equal lots. In one, mix *oboro*; in another scrambled egg; in the last snow peas.
**5.** Cut *nori* in half vertically.
**6.** Lay 1 strip of *nori* across the rolling mat lengthwise. Make a belt-like pattern across the center of *nori* with ⅙ of the sushi rice mixed with *oboro*. Use the mat to fold *nori* over rice, and press to form a conelike shape. Repeat the process for 5 more *oboro*-filled rolls, and for 6 rolls of scrambled egg and 6 of snow peas.
**7.** Line up the rolls one above the other, alternating them according to their contents. Cut into 4 equal parts with a knife dampened in rice vinegar. Cut again into halves. Arrange on a tray or plate like a cluster of a wisteria, with the cut edges showing.

**6 Servings**
**Cooking time: 30 minutes**

3 pounds (1.4 kg) sushi rice
½ thick omelet
8 ounces (200 g) gourd strips,
    seasoned
1 cup *oboro* (whitefish flakes)
10 mushrooms, seasoned
8 bunches spinach
    Small amount of soy sauce
4 sheets *yaki-nori* (toasted
    seaweed)
Rice vinegar for wetting fingers
    and dampening the knife

**6 Servings**
**Cooking time: 30 minutes**

3 pounds (1.4 kg) sushi rice
½ thick omelet
4 pieces *narazuke**. Pickles may
    be used as a substitute
    * They are Japanese pickles. It
    is a pickled cucumber in rice
    wine dregs.
8 bunches spinach
    Small amount of soy sauce
4 sheets *yaki-nori* (toasted
    seaweed)
Rice vinegar for wetting fingers
    and dampening the knife

# *Futo-Maki-*Zushi (Thick Sushi Rolls)

For regular sushi rolls, only half a sheet of *nori* is used to roll but in this case a whole sheet is used.

| Calories 499 | Protein 11.4 g | Fats 1.4 g | Carbohydrates 110.2 g |
|---|---|---|---|

**1.** See "How to Cook Basic Sushi Ingredients" on pages 70 to 73 and prepare sushi rice, thick omelet, seasoned gourd strips, *oboro* and seasoned mushrooms.
**2.** Slice omelet into strips, making sure the length does not exceed the width of *nori*. Cut gourd strips to the same length. Slice mushrooms ⅕ inch (0.5 cm) thick.
**3.** Boil spinach. Immerse in ice water and squeeze out firmly to release water as much as possible. Sprinkle on a small amount of soy sauce and set aside.
**4.** Place one sheet of *nori* on the rolling mat vertically. Wet fingers and palms with vinegar and spread ¼ of sushi rice onto *nori*, leaving 1-inch (2.5-cm) blank across the top of the sheet. Starting from a little this side of the center of the rice, lay ¼ each of the following items across it horizontally: omelet and gourd strips, *oboro*, mushrooms and spinach. Roll into a cylinder-like shape keeping the edges even. Repeat the process for the other three rolls.
**5.** Set the rolls aside to allow them to firm up, with the crease in *nori* on the bottom. Cut each roll into 8 equal parts, cleaning and dampening the knife with vinegar. Garnish with sweet-and-sour ginger, if desired.

# *Ura-Maki-*Zushi (Inside-Out Rolls)

This is a different type of sushi roll, with sushi rice on the outside and *nori* inside. This type requires a little practice to make.

| Calories 489 | Protein 10.8 g | Fats 1.3 g | Carbohydrates 104 g |
|---|---|---|---|

**1.** See "How to Cook Basic Sushi Ingredients" on pages 70 to 73 and prepare sushi rice and thick omelet.
**2.** Cut omelet and *narazuke* into cylinder shapes about the thickness of a pencil making sure not to cut them larger than the width of *nori*.
**3.** Boil spinach. Immerse in ice water and squeeze out firmly to release as much water as possible. Sprinkle on a small amount of soy sauce and set aside.
**4.** Unfold a sheet of *nori*, placing it vertically on the rolling mat. Wet your fingers and palms with the vinegar and spread ¼ of sushi rice over *nori* evenly. Cover with the saran wrap and press evenly.
**5.** Turn over so that *nori* is now on top and the saran wrap is on the mat. Lay ¼ of omelet, *narazuke* and spinach horizontally across the end of *nori* closest to you. Roll almost one complete turn, stopping to press and make firm, then complete the roll. Dampen the knife with rice vinegar and cut the roll into slices 1 inch (2.5 cm) thick. Gently remove the saran wrap. Repeat the process for the remaining sheets of *nori*.

●*Konbu-Maki* (**Sushi Rolled in** *Konbu*) . . . **See page 73.**

# *Ebi-Oshi*-Zushi (Sushi Sunburst with Shrimps)

Line a sponge cake baking pan with saran wrap. Fillet the boiled shrimp so that they will lie flat and then place them in a sunburst pattern. Smear a dab of *wasabi* on shrimp.

Put sushi rice on the top of shrimp. When the pan is filled half-way with sushi rice, and *yaki-nori*. Then, add sushi rice again on *yaki-nori* and press firmly.

Turn the pan over and allow the ingredients to fall into a plate. Not only is it easier to cut but also prevents sushi from crumbling when the saran wrap is left on.

# Tsubaki-Zushi (Camellia-Blossom Sushi)
# Saba-Zushi (Mackerel Sushi)
# Tazuna-Zushi (Striated Sushi Bars)

**4 Servings**
**Cooking time: 45 minutes**

3 pounds (1.4 kg) sushi rice
16 medium-size shrimps
   3 tablespoons rice vinegar
   1 tablespoon sugar
   ½ teaspoon salt
2 sheets *yaki-nori* (toasted
   seaweed)
Small amount of powdered or
   freshly grated *wasabi* (Japanese
   green horseradish)
10 leaves green *shiso* (beefsteak
   plant)

# *Ebi-Oshi*-Zushi
## (Sushi Sunburst with Shrimps)

This is pressed sushi molded in a cake pan. A 7-inch (17.5-cm) deep cake pan is used here.

| Calories 696 | Protein 31.4 g | Fats 2.2 g | Carbohydrates 145.2 g |
|---|---|---|---|

1. See "How to Cook Basic Sushi Ingredients" on page 70 and prepare sushi rice.
2. Devein shrimps and remove the head. Run a bamboo skewer through the abdomen up to the tail. Cook in lightly vinegared boiling water for about 3 minutes. Remove to a strainer and let cool. When cool, rotate the skewer to pull off shrimps. Remove the shell and tail.
3. Make a shallow slit down shrimps on the abdomen side and gently spread shrimps apart but keeping the two parts connected. Sprinkle with vinegar, sugar and salt, and let sit for 20 minutes.
4. Line a deep cake pan with the saran wrap, leaving a little of it hanging over the edge. Place shrimps on the saran wrap, abdomen-side up, in a sunburst pattern, much like the spokes on a tire. Smear a dab of *wasabi* on each shrimp. Spread half sushi rice evenly over shrimps. Cover with *yaki-nori* and press down firmly. Spread the remainder of the rice evenly over *yaki-nori*. Cover with an extra piece of saran wrap and press down firmly.
5. Layer a plate with green *shiso*. Turn the rice cake over and place on. Remove the saran wrap and cut into wedges to eat.

**4 Servings**
**Cooking time: 45 minutes**

1¾ pounds (800 g) sushi rice
1 block (7 ounces = 175 g) raw
   tuna, red meat
1 block (6 ounces = 150 g) raw
   flatfish
1 egg yolk, hard boiled
Small amount of powdered or
   freshly grated *wasabi* (Japanese
   green horseradish)

# *Tsubaki*-Zushi (Camellia-Blossom Sushi)

As the name implies, this is a kind of sushi which resembles the shape of a flower. It can be made easily at home.

| Calories 459 | Protein 28.2 g | Fats 3.9 g | Carbohydrates 77.8 g |
|---|---|---|---|

1. See "How to Cook Basic Sushi Ingredients" on page 70 and prepare sushi rice.
2. Make about 20 small round balls from sushi rice.
3. Thinly slice tuna and flatfish into 2-inch (5-cm) squares.
4. Mash the yolk with the back of a spoon.
5. Wet and thoroughly wring dry a small dish cloth. In the center, place 1 slice of fish, smear on a dab of *wasabi* and top with 1 rice ball. Gather the corners of the cloth to make an upside-down parachute, and twist to set the rice against the fish and turn over. With your finger, make a dimple in the fish through the cloth. Unwrap carefully and place on a plate. Dab a bit of the yolk into the dimple.
6. Repeat the process for each rice ball. If desired, place each "blossom" on a real camellia leaf. Dip in soy sauce to eat.

# *Saba*-Zushi (Mackerel Sushi)

Simple but excellent sushi. It is important that only the freshest mackerel be used.

| Calories 560 | Protein 23.5 g | Fats 15.6 g | Carbohydrates 81.4 g |
|---|---|---|---|

1. See "How to Cook Basic Sushi Ingredients" on page 70 and

**4 Servings**
**Cooking time: 45 minutes, plus
  salting and marinating time**

1¾ pounds (800 g) sushi rice
1 mackerel, whole
    Salt and rice vinegar
    1 cup rice vinegar
    1 tablespoon sugar
2 sheets *shiraita-konbu* (a dried
    white kelp sheet)
Small amount of rice vinegar,
    sugar, salt
½ ounce (14 g) ginger

**Note:** *Shiraita-konbu* is
indispensable to Mackerel Sushi,
but, if it is not available, use
*oboro-konbu* (thinly sliced kelp)
instead. Or, it can be made
without using either of these
ingredients.

**4 Servings**
**Cooking time: 45 minutes, plus
  salting and marinating time**

2¼ pounds (1 kg) sushi rice
8 *kisu* (sillago), whole
    1 scant tablespoon salt
    rice vinegar
12 medium-size shrimps
Small amount of vinegar for
    boiling water
    3 tablespoons rice vinegar
    1½ tablespoons sugar
    ½ teaspoon salt
1 slender cucumber
    ¼ teaspoon salt
Small amount of sweet-and-sour
    ginger
Small amount of powdered or
    freshly grated *wasabi* (Japanese
    green horseradish)

Spread a sheet of saran wrap on the
rolling bamboo mat and line up ¼ of
the shrimps, cucumber and *kisu*
(sillago) alternately side by side.

prepare sushi rice.

**2.** Fillet mackerel on both sides and throw away the bony section.
Slice off small bones around abdominal cavity of the 2 filleted pieces.
Coat both sides of the fillets heavily with salt. Let stand for 3 to 4
hours.

**3.** Rinse off salt with rice vinegar in the bowl, and remove any
remaining bones in the dark meat. Peel off skin, starting from the
head. Combine 1 cup of vinegar with 1 tablespoon sugar and marinate the fillets for 30 minutes.

**4.** Combine *konbu* with small amount of vinegar, sugar and salt,
plus water to cover. Cook for about 5 minutes and then allow to cool.

**5.** Peel ginger, cut into needle-thin pieces and soak in water.

**6.** Spread a sheet of the saran wrap on the rolling mat. Place one
fillet on it skin side down. Sprinkle half sliced ginger on the fillet. Use
½ of the rice and make a rough bar and lay across the fillet. Roll the
rolling mat one complete turn, pause and press firmly. Roll back the
saran wrap. Lay 1 piece of *konbu* across the fillet. Roll with the saran
wrap again, allowing time for the flavor to penetrate.

**7.** Remove the saran wrap and cut into slices 1 inch (2.5 cm) thick.
Set out sweet-and-sour ginger as garnish, as you like. Dip in soy sauce
to eat.

# *Tazuna*-Zushi (Striated Sushi Bars)

*Tazuna-zushi* is characterized by its tricolored rope pattern of red,
green and white materials. Not only making but also eating *tazuna-
zushi* is a delightful experience.

| Calories 558 | Protein 32.7 g | Fats 2.7 g | Carbohydrates 100.7 g |
|---|---|---|---|

**1.** See "How to Cook Basic Sushi Ingredients" on page 70, and
prepare sushi rice.

**2.** Fillet *kisu* on both sides, and throw away the bony section. Cut
vertically into halves if it is large. Sprinkle 2 or 4 fillets with salt and let
stand for 1 hour. Rinse off salt by dipping *kisu* in vinegar. Remove any
remaining bones. Peel off the skin, starting from the head. Soak in
vinegar and marinate for 15 minutes.

**3.** Devein each shrimp and remove the head. Run a bamboo
skewer through the abdomen up to the tail. Bring the lightly vinegared water to a boil. Boil shrimps for 2 minutes, then allow to cool.
Remove the skewer when cool and shell. Remove the tail. Cut each
shrimp lengthwise into two pieces. Marinate in the combined vinegar, sugar and salt for about 20 minutes.

**4.** Cut cucumber in half and slice thinly lengthwise into long strips.
Remove all seeds if they are hard. Sprinkle cucumber sticks with salt
and let stand long enough to make soft and pliable.

**5.** Cut sweet-and-sour ginger into needle-thin pieces.

**6.** Spread a sheet of the saran wrap on the rolling mat. Line up ¼ of
*kisu*, cucumber and shrimps, alternating them as you make a belt
across the wrap starting from the left end, with the ingredients being
placed on a slightly diagonal angle. Smear with a dab of *wasabi*.
Sprinkle on some of ginger. Form ¼ of sushi rice into a rough bar and
place on top. Roll almost one complete turn with the rolling mat.
Pause to press and firm. Finish the roll so that the ingredients are on
top. Allow to set for a moment. Unroll mat, and bind both ends of the
sushi bars. After cutting into slices about 1½ inches (4 cm) thick,
remove the saran wrap. Repeat the process for the remainder.

# Four Types of Sushi Making with Eggs

## *Chakin*-Zushi (Sushi Pods) *Fukusa*-Zushi (Sushi Cushion) *Hamaguri*-Zushi (Clamshell-Like Sushi) *Date-Maki*-Zushi (Egg-Roll Sushi)

Place one mound of sushi rice mixture in the center of a wafer-thin omelet.

Gather the four corners to wrap sushi rice. Be careful not to tear omelet.

Use two strips of blanched *mitsuba* to tie the tips together. Do not tie too tight, or omelet will tear.

Shape the pod. Leave an opening at the top of the pod so that sushi rice can be seen slightly. Fill this opening with *oboro*.

# *Inari*-Zushi (Sushi Pouches)

Turn the upper half (on the open side) of the *abura-age* pouch inside out, and put in a ball of sushi rice mixture.

When the pouch is filled halfway, lift the end of the other side, and push the front side inside the pouch.

Pulling the end of the other side, cover and shape the sushi well. Serve it with the over-lapped sides underneath.

**4 Servings**
**Cooking time: 30 minutes**

1¾ pounds (800 g) sushi rice
12 wafer-thin omelets 6 inches by
   6 inches (15 cm by 15 cm)
4 ounces (100 g) gourd strips,
   seasoned
4 ounces (100 g) carrots,
   seasoned
⅔ cup *oboro* (whitefish flakes)
24 leaves *mitsuba* (trefoil), long
1 sheet *yaki-nori* (toasted
   seaweed)

# *Chakin*-Zushi (Sushi Pods)

This sushi is called *chakin-zushi* in Japanese. *Chakin* is a small piece of cloth used for the traditional Japanese tea ceremony. Omelets should be just as thin as this cloth.

| Calories 656 | Protein 22.0 g | Fats 15.8 g | Carbohydrates 106.5 g |
|---|---|---|---|

**1.** See "How to Cook Basic Sushi Ingredients" on pages 70 to 72 and prepare sushi rice, wafer-thin omelets, seasoned gourd strips, seasoned carrots and *oboro*.
**2.** Chop gourd strips and carrots finely. Place *yaki-nori* in a plastic bag and crumple into fine pieces.
**3.** Blanch *mitsuba* a few seconds, put into ice water and then drain.
**4.** Mix gourd strips, carrots and *yaki-nori* into the sushi rice. Form the mixture into 12 equal mounds.
**5.** Place one mound of rice on each omelet. Gather the four corners forming a rough pod. Tie the tips together loosely with *mitsuba*. Gently fold open the four "pockets" of the "leaves" and fill lightly with *oboro*. Repeat the process for the remaining pods. (See technique photos on page 86).

**4 Servings**
**Cooking time: 30 minutes**

1¾ pounds (800 g) sushi rice
12 wafer-thin omelets 6 inches by
   6 inches (15 cm by 15 cm)
7 ounces (175 g) gourd strips,
   seasoned
4 ounces (100 g) carrots,
   seasoned
1 sheet *yaki-nori* (toasted
   seaweed)

# *Fukusa*-Zushi (Sushi Cushion)

Another wonderful idea for making sushi with wafer-thin omelets. It's fun, decorative and appealing to mix all kinds of colorful ingredients into sushi rice.

| Calories 658 | Protein 21.8 g | Fats 15.2 g | Carbohydrates 108.6 g |
|---|---|---|---|

**1.** See "How to Cook Basic Sushi Ingredients" on pages 70 to 73 and prepare sushi rice, wafer-thin omelets, seasoned gourd strips and seasoned carrots.
**2.** Finely chop half gourd strips and all carrots. Place *yaki-nori* in a plastic bag and crumple into fine pieces.
**3.** Mix gourd strips, carrots, *yaki-nori* into sushi rice. Form 12 patties in a rough square shape.
**4.** Place one patty in the center of each omelet. Wrap sushi rice as shown in the picture (page 86). Tie the "cushion" with one of gourd strips.
**5.** Decorate with salted young rape blossoms or other garnishes if desired.

**4 Servings**
**Cooking time: 30 minutes**

1⅓ pounds (600 g) sushi rice
7 eggs
   2 tablespoons sugar
   1 teaspoon salt

# *Hamaguri*-Zushi (Clamshell-Like Sushi)

An ingenious idea of sushi making which can be done at home. Serve it together with Sushi Cushion as shown in the picture on page 86 and you'll get a wonderful result.

| Calories 452 | Protein 16.2 g | Fats 10.7 g | Carbohydrates 72.7 g |
|---|---|---|---|

**1.** See "How to Cook Basic Sushi Ingredients" on pages 70 to 73 and prepare sushi rice, seasoned carrots, seasoned burdock shavings.
**2.** Mix eggs for Wafer-Thin Omelets (see page 72) but cook each in 7-inch (17.5-cm) round frying pan, making 12 in all.
**3.** Remove all stems from snow peas. Cook in salted, boiling water.

2 teaspoons potato starch or
   cornstarch
3 ounces (75 g) julienned carrots,
   seasoned
2 ounces (50 g) burdock shavings,
   seasoned
12 snow peas

After immersing in ice water, drain and slice into needle-thin pieces.
**4.** Mix carrots, burdock shavings and snow peas with sushi rice. Divide into 12 equal parts.
**5.** Place one portion of the rice on one omelet, evenly, on one side. Make 4 folds, starting with the bottom to make the crêpe.
**6.** Heat a metal skewer until red hot, and make 3 decorative marks on the "neck" of the "shell". Repeat the process for the remaining omelets.

**6 Servings**
**Cooking time: 30 minutes**

2¼ pounds (1 kg) sushi rice
4 thick omelets
12 long carrot sticks, seasoned,
   cut ⅕ inch by ⅕ inch (0.5 cm
   by 0.5 cm)
10' mushrooms, seasoned
6 ounces (150 g) gourd strips,
   seasoned

# Date-Maki-Zushi (Egg-Roll Sushi)

This is a luxurious rolled sushi called *Date-Maki*-Zushi in Japanese. "Date" gives the impression of being dandy in appearance.

| Calories 639 | Protein 26.1 g | Fats 16.0 g | Carbohydrates 97.8 g |
|---|---|---|---|

**1.** See "How to Cook Basic Sushi Ingredients" on pages 70 to 73 and prepare sushi rice, thick omelet, seasoned carrots, seasoned mushrooms and seasoned gourd strips.
**2.** Cut carrots and gourd strips to lengths that do not exceed the width of omelet. Slice mushrooms ¼ inch (0.5 cm) thick.
**3.** Place one omelet on the rolling mat. Spread ¼ of sushi rice evenly over omelet. Across the center of the rice, horizontally lay ¼ of carrots, gourd strips and mushrooms. Pick up the nearest and farthest edges of the mat and roll it almost one complete turn. Pause to check edges of omelet are aligned. Press firmly to set, then finish rolling. Repeat the process for the remaining 3 omelets.
**4.** Once the rolls have been set, cut into slices 1 inch (2.5 cm) thick.

**4 Servings**
**Cooking time: 45 minutes**

2 pounds (900 g) sushi rice
4 ounces (100 g) burdock
   shavings, seasoned
4 ounces (100 g) carrots,
   julienned and seasoned
8 pieces *abura-age* (deep-fried
   *tofu*)
   6 tablespoons sugar
   2⅔ tablespoons soy sauce
   1½ cups *dashi*
3 tablespoons white sesame seeds
   (toasted)

# Inari-Zushi (Sushi Pouches)

This is one of the vegetable types also referred to as *kitsune* (fox)-zushi. In Japan, *abura-age* is considered a fox's favorite food.

| Calories 799 | Protein 21.6 g | Fats 25.6 g | Carbohydrates 120.6 g |
|---|---|---|---|

**1.** See "How to Cook Basic Sushi Ingredients" on pages 70 to 73 and prepare sushi rice, *dashi*, seasoned burdock shavings and seasoned carrots.
**2.** Cut each *abura-age* in half. Open each section into a pouch. Remove any excess oil by boiling in water for 1 to 2 minutes.
**3.** Combine *dashi*, sugar and soy sauce in a pan and bring to a boil. Add the pouches, cover with a Japanese-style wooden lid that is placed directly on the food. If you do not have one, make holes in a sheet of aluminum foil and use it instead, and simmer over low heat for 20 minutes. Let cool in the pan.
**4.** Mix sushi rice, burdock shavings, carrots and sesame seeds. Shape roughly into 16 lots and set aside.
**5.** Stuff half the pouches with some of the rice mixture, leaving space for the opening to be folded over into a flap. Turn the other half of the pouches inside out and stuff.
**Note:** Additional ways to use the pouches:
(1) Fold down the edges of the pouch inward about ½-inch (1 cm), like a basket, and fill so the rice can be seen.
(2) Fill the pouch, but turn down the flaps so that the pouch takes on a pyramid or diamond shape.

# Sushi and Health

## Sushi as Low-Calorie Food

It is now common knowledge that sushi is a low-calorie food when compared with Western-style food and that it is more healthy and does not add on any extra unwanted pounds.

Oil is used for almost all European and American dishes, but hardly any oil is used in the making of sushi. Now, let us take a look at what difference there is in the calorie content between dishes prepared without oil and those which are cooked with oil.

Here you can see a small calorie table of dishes each of which weighing 4 ounces (100 g). The calculations were made only for foods made and marketed in Japan.

| | |
|---|---|
| Hand-formed tuna sushi (red meat) | 148 kcal |
| *Chirashi*-zushi | 136 kcal |
| Chinese dish of fried rice (*chao-fan*) | 187 kcal |
| Fried chicken | 257 kcal |
| Mix pizza | 311 kcal |

The calorific value of sushi is far lower than that of fried chicken or pizza. The difference between the calorific value of sushi and that of *chao-fan*, both of which use rice, is due to whether oil is used for cooking.

However, it is too much to say that all Japanese dishes are healthy, low-calorie dishes. For instance, salt is an essential seasoning for Japanese dishes, and needless to say, an excessive intake of it is not at all good for one's health. Sushi contains salt in various forms. It is contained not only in sushi rice and soy sauce but also in some sushi-*dane*, to which salt is added in the seasoning process. The more you eat sushi, the more you take salt, so it is needless to say that you had better not overeat sushi.

By the way, Japanese tea which is served at sushi shops (see page 28) has an unexpected, delightful effect. Japanese tea has hardly any calorific value and contains only a small amount of kalium, which serves to discharge salt from one's body. Japanese tea is, in this respect, a drink particularly suited to sushi and other types of Japanese dishes.

## Sushi as Balanced Food

In Japanese cooking, all dishes are cooked so that they contained five basic tastes—sourness, bitterness, sweetness, hotness and saltiness. Thus, in the case of hand-formed *toro* sushi, sourness is given by vinegar in sushi rice, saltiness by soy sauce and as a result of the salt contained in sushi rice, sweetness by the taste from chewed rice and melty sweetness of the *toro* meat, bitterness in soy sauce

**Nutritional Content of Different Dishes**

| Contents \ Dishes | *Nigiri*-Zushi (red meat of tuna) | *Chirashi*-Zushi | Fried Chicken | Mix Pizza | *Chao-Fan* |
|---|---|---|---|---|---|
| Quantity (g) | 42 | 489.2 | 145 | 187.4 | 374 |
| Calories (kcal) | 62 | 665 | 373 | 582 | 700 |
| Protein (g) | 4.2 | 30.5 | 19.1 | 21.9 | 22.3 |
| Fats (g) | 0.3 | 8.2 | 22.2 | 23.8 | 31.9 |
| Sugar (g) | 9.7 | 110.3 | 20.3 | 64.6 | 74.2 |
| Calcium (mg) | 1 | 67 | 34 | 291 | 66 |
| Phosphorus (mg) | 43 | 352 | 115 | 329 | 271 |
| Iron (mg) | 0.3 | 2.4 | 1 | 1.5 | 2.3 |
| Sodium (mg) | 135 | 2738 | 722 | 775 | 1095 |
| Potassium (mg) | 59 | 430 | 237 | 286 | 341 |
| Vitamin A (IU) | 2 | 303 | 263 | 506 | 348 |
| Vitamin $B_1$ (mg) | 0.02 | 0.19 | 0.09 | 0.27 | 0.39 |
| Vitamin $B_2$ (mg) | 0.01 | 0.33 | 0.13 | 0.28 | 0.39 |
| Vitamin C (mg) | 0.24 | 2 | 2 | 13 | 8 |
| Salt (g) | 0.3 | 7 | 1.8 | 2 | 2.8 |
| Calories per 100 g (kcal) | 147.6 | 136.0 | 257.2 | 310.6 | 187.2 |

and bitterness and hotness given by Japanese horseradish (*wasabi*). Slight bitterness and hotness are essential for really refined Japanese dishes in order to harmonize and balance the entire taste of the dish.

It is said that the cooks who served the *Tokugawa* Shogunates, never failed to use a grain of bitter seasonings for all dishes served. They paid a very dear price to obtain the gall of a bear so as to give the proper amount of bitterness to the food served.

Not only in Japan but in China as well great medical importance is attached to these five tastes. In China, the important internal organs of the body are called the five viscera, which are seen as corresponding to the five tastes. The five viscera are liver, heart, spleen, kidneys and lungs, which are thought to correspond to the tastes of sourness, bitterness, sweetness, saltiness and hotness, respectively. For instance, it is said that when one organ becomes weak, it regains vitality if the taste corresponding to that organ is given. Furthermore, it was thought that conversely, if any of these tastes is supplied in excess, the corresponding organ will become ill. This system of the five viscera corresponding to the five tastes is found in *Su-Wen*, a classic regarding Oriental medicine. Though not scientifically founded, this system, based on experience, appears to contain something that cannot be simply discarded.

In China, it has been said that medicine and eating come from the same root, or medicine and food are of a kind. This means that each dish should contain these five tastes, and that if one eats such a dish, one will always remain in good health.

Sushi is a very healthy food which contains all these five tastes.

## Sushi and Prevention of Adult's Diseases

Sushi is made by combining sushi rice with various kinds of *tane* or *gu*. Leaving aside sushi rice, we will study the relationships between *tane* or *gu* and diseases related to adults.

Sushi shops offer fish meat called shining *tane*. Such fish are generally slim and have blue-shining backs. The most common of the fish are sardines and mackerels. The oil which is contained in such fish, has a large content of highly unsaturated fatty acid, called EPA, which works to prevent such adult-related diseases as cerebral thrombosis and myocardial infarction, diseases whose incidence is very high in highly civilized societies.

The temperature of human beings and other animals which live on land is maintained at more or less at a constant level so that the oil in the body does not coagulate. However, sardines and mackerels whose body temperatures are not maintained at a constant level have fat which does not coagulate even at low temperatures so that they can live in cold waters, and their fat has a large content of EPA which is effective for preventing cerebral thrombosis.

Furthermore, recent studies have shown that fish, octopus, cuttlefish and shellfish have taurine, an amino acid, which is known to be effective for lowering the cholesterol level in blood and preventing arterial sclerosis.

Among various kinds of shellfish, there are shellfish which contain both taurine and cholesterol. It is said that octopus, cuttlefish and other mollusks have a fairly high content of cholesterol, and even Japanese hesitate to eat them. However, these contain not only cholesterol but also taurine, with the taurine being as much as eight times the amount of cholesterol. Naturally, the taurine these fish possess is more effective and healthy than cholesterol.

The fish and shellfish that have a relatively high content of taurine, are hairy crab, oyster, octopus, short-necked clam, horse-neck clam, bonito, and yellowtail. (See table on page 93).

## Rice and Blood Sugar Levels

Let me digress a little. When one gets hungry, you sometimes find that you easily get angry or irritated. At such a time you can overcome this irritation temporarily if you eat something. This is directly related to the blood sugar level.

If you eat food with a high sugar content, sugar is absorbed quickly in the upper part of the small intestine to be turned into grape sugar and raises your blood sugar level sharply. Then, insulin is secreted to lower the blood sugar level. As a result, the blood sugar level drops suddenly. It drops so sharply that it reaches a level lower than it was before you had something to eat. In this state of a low blood sugar level, you feel giddy, perspire, get irritated and suffer from palpitation and lack of concentration, or from conditions unfavorable for the carrying out of your work. Therefore, eating something sweet to overcome irritation actually has the opposite effect.

Some time ago, I conducted blood sugar level tests for three weeks on seven university students.

In the first week, they were made to eat rice with a certain calorific value. In the next week, they were made to eat bread with the same calorific value, and in the third week, they ate sugar with the same calorific value. The experiment showed that when they were given sugar, they showed a remarkably high blood sugar level after 30 minutes and their blood sugar level fell below the lowest blood sugar level (100) they showed before they ate sugar, and reached an extremely low level of 50 in 2 hours. Conversely, when they ate rice, their blood sugar level rose a little in 30 minutes, but their blood sugar level remained about the same (100) as it was before they ate rice after 1 or 2 hours. (See table below).

The reason for this change is that sugar and bread are powdered-type foods while rice is eaten in grain form. Rice grains take time to be digested, and is absorbed slowly in the form of grape sugar from the intestine to raise the blood sugar level slowly. Therefore, the blood sugar level of those who eat rice is more stable.

The relationship between health and Japanese dishes including sushi is unthinkable without the function of rice, which is basic to Japanese foods and sushi, to stabilize the blood sugar level. The Japanese, whose staple food is rice, do not feel hungry between meals and do not take light meals between them, and so do not become over-weight. They have more concentration and can work until noon without the necessity of taking a coffee break in the morning.

## Sushi and A Healthy Way of Eating

While Asian people, including the Japanese, do not tend to become fat, Americans and Europeans on the whole do have a tendency to be overweight. It is said that this is because of their excessive intake of fat, but I think that is not the only reason.

**Normal Patterns of Changes in Blood Sugar Levels after Eating Carbohydrates**

| Time (m) / Foods | 0 | 30 | 60 | 90 | 120 |
|---|---|---|---|---|---|
| Rice | 100 | 146 | 117 | 112 | 108 |
| Bread | 100 | 129 | 67 | 79 | 92 |
| Sugar | 100 | 283 | 167 | 105 | 50 |

It is said that Japanese and other Asians are clever with their fingers, and the use of chopsticks is cited as an example to show this. It seems to me that the fact that Asians use chopsticks in eating food has something to do with the fact that they do not become too fat. Now let's consider not what we eat but how we eat it.

There is a definite difference in the eating time between when you eat curried rice or piraffe with a spoon and when you eat a Japanese dish using chopsticks. It takes more time to eat using chopsticks. It takes foreigners even more time than Japanese when chopsticks are employed. About 5 to 7 minutes would be enough for you to eat two hamburgers and drink a bottle of cola. By so doing you would consume at least 800 to 900 kilo calories in a very short time. Suppose that you went to a sushi bar and order sushi, a bowl of *miso* soup, pickles and a small dish or relish. This sushi course would be lower in calorific value by more than 200 kilo calories than two hamburgers and a bottle of cola. It will take about 1 hour to finish this course if eaten properly, or 10 times more time that when you eat two hamburgers and drink a bottle of cola.

The appetite nerve center of the brain has a satiety center and a hunger center, and it is grape sugar in the blood that sends signals to these nerve centers. It seems that it takes time for the grape sugar to be carried by blood and reach the satiety center of the brain. If you finish eating food in a short time, you do not feel satisfied and tend to eat to excess, with the result that you take in more calories than your body needs. So, how about eating daily foods with chopsticks or the like and reducing a calorie intake by allowing more time to consume them.

Another healthy way of eating is to eat food pleasantly in an agreeable atmosphere. You can digest food better in this way. Communication between sushi makers and customers is also an important factor for eating freshly formed sushi in a pleasant mood. You had better start eating newly formed sushi as quickly as possible. Otherwise, you will not be able to get the pleasant feeling of biting into properly warmed sushi. It would be very good to ask a sushi-maker about the *tane* he can recommend. Communication with the sushi-maker starts there, and the sushi-maker will do everything he can to make good-tasting sushi. Take time to eat freshly formed sushi in a pleasant mood. This is the healthy and pleasant way of eating sushi.

# Seafood with A High Content of Taurine

Taurine is contained more in muscles, liver, brain and other parts. It is also contained in livestock animal meat, too, but it also has a high content of cholesterol. In the case of beef, the ratio of taurine to cholesterol is 1.0 for meat fit for roasting, and 0.2 for liver. An adult's daily intake of taurine from food is estimated at about 100 mg.

| Seafood \ Item | Taurine content (mg/100 g) | Cholesterol content (mg/100 g) | Ratio = Taurine / Cholesterol | Remarks |
|---|---|---|---|---|
| Sardine | 175.7 | 49.6 | 3.5 | The edible part of the fish is sliced thin and the slices are mixed well so that differences in the measurement values of taurine according to different parts might be reduced to a minimum. 10 grams of the mixed slices is used as a sample (hereafter the same). Since this fish is a low in cost, it should be used more as sushi-*dane*. |
| Yellowtail (bloody meat) | 672.9 | 32.9 | 20.5 | Yellowtail meat, including the bloody part, has a taurine content of 187 mg/100 g, cholesterol content of 37 mg/100 g and a ratio of about 5.0. |
| (ordinary meat) | 15.7 | 42.8 | 0.4 | |
| Bonito (bloody meat) | 832.0 | 79.9 | 10.4 | Bonito meat, including the bloody part, has a taurine content of 163 mg/100 g with a cholesterol content of 43 mg/100 g, with its ratio being 3.9. |
| (ordinary meat) | 2.6 | 17.5 | 0.1 | |
| Sea Bream | 192.9 | 48.3 | 4.0 | White-meat fish have only a small amount of taurine, the content only being 60 mg/100 g with a ratio of 1.7 for *gin-dara* (silvery cod). However, sea bream has a relatively high content of taurine. |
| Horse Mackerel | 228.9 | 48.8 | 4.7 | *Ma-aji* (horse mackerel) is a familiar fish, but today it is considered to be high-class fish. Recently, horse mackerels caught in the sea are refrigerated before they reach the marketplace in Japan. |
| Mackerel | 168.0 | 47.5 | 3.5 | The taurine-cholesterol ratio of meat of blue-fish averages 3.5—4.0, and this meat also has a high content of fatty acid called EPA, which is said to be effective for preventing arterial sclerosis. |
| Horse-Neck Clam | 730.4 | 40.0 | 18.3 | *Uni* (sea urchin), a familiar *tane* at sushi shops, has more cholesterol than taurine. When you order *uni*-sushi, never fail to order shellfish sushi at the same time. |
| Octopus | 537.5 | 96.1 | 5.6 | Some people say that the broth from octopus is very effective for alleviating inflammation and that it is effective when used as a gurgling solution. Maybe this is due to the taurine they contain. |
| Squid | 364.1 | 166.1 | 2.2 | Squid has a high content of both cholesterol and taurine. The taurine-cholesterol content ratio is more than 2.2 for both *yari-ika* and *mongo-ika*. |
| Short-Necked Clam | 421.0 | 52.3 | 8.0 | All shellfish have an extremely high content of taurine, the content per 100 g being 550 mg for clams and 670 mg for the eyes of scallop. However, the content is unexpectedly low for corbicula living in fresh water. |
| Oyster | 490.6 | 39.1 | 12.5 | The following figure shows taurine content in packed oyster. In the case of oyster in its shell without any natural juice, the taurine content is 1,178 mg/100 g. |
| Hairy Crab | 37.3 | 69.7 | 5.4 | This figure shows taurine in a hairy crab boiled in its shell. Canned crab meat also has a fairly high content of taurine, and some part of it is exuded into the juice in the canned crab meat. The juice should not be discarded for it adds to and complements crab meat. |

# Main Kinds of Sushi and Their Distribution in Japan

**Note 1:** Names of prefectures are in boldface.
**Note 2:** As for sushi types not mentioned here, refer to pages 10 to 15.

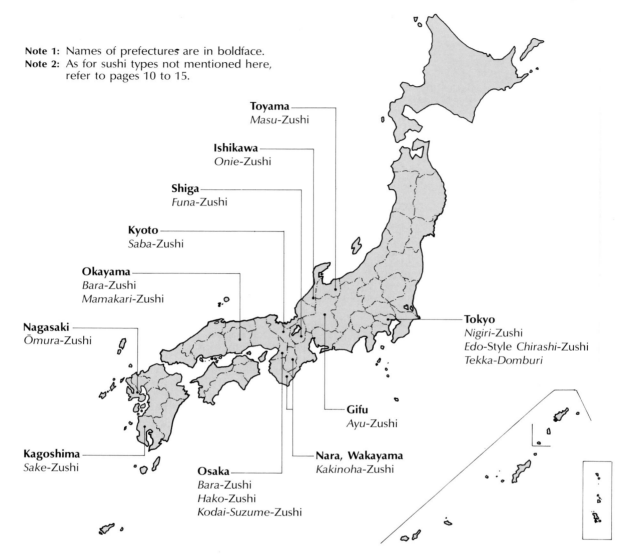

**Toyama**
*Masu*-Zushi

**Ishikawa**
*Onie*-Zushi

**Shiga**
*Funa*-Zushi

**Kyoto**
*Saba*-Zushi

**Okayama**
*Bara*-Zushi
*Mamakari*-Zushi

**Nagasaki**
*Ōmura*-Zushi

**Kagoshima**
*Sake*-Zushi

**Osaka**
*Bara*-Zushi
*Hako*-Zushi
*Kodai-Suzume*-Zushi

**Nara, Wakayama**
*Kakinoha*-Zushi

**Gifu**
*Ayu*-Zushi

**Tokyo**
*Nigiri*-Zushi
*Edo*-Style *Chirashi*-Zushi
*Tekka-Domburi*

● *Funa*-Zushi **(Shiga)** A kind of *nare-zushi* using crucian carp with roe. The oldest existing type of sushi.
● *Masu*-Zushi **(Toyama)** Thinly sliced trout meat is laid on sushi rice in two alternate layers. This is kept as it is for one day so as to allow it to ferment. It is said that it dates back to 1717.
● *Ayu*-Zushi **(Gifu)** This is a kind of *nama-nare*-zushi (fermented sushi) made by cormorant fishermen on the Nagara River toward the end of September every year. This sushi is served on the New Year's day as a special treat.
● *Onie*-Zushi **(Ishikawa)** "Onie" means an offering to the gods. This sushi is a kind of *oshi*-zushi made at the time of the spring and autumn festivals. It is said that originally

fishermen made this type of sushi using fish as "*gu*" as a prayer to the gods for big hauls of fish.
● *Kakinoha*-Zushi **(Nara and Waka-yama)** Sushi rice balls are formed, and salted mackerel or salted salmon which have been fermented in vinegar, are put on them, which are then wrapped in persimmon tree leaves and are pressed under a weight.
● *Bara*-Zushi **(Okayama)** A very sumptuous *chirashi*-zushi peculiar to this district. This sushi is made on the day of the spring festival.
● *Mamakari*-Zushi **(Okayama)** This district is known for this sushi as well as for its *chirashi*-zushi. *Mamakari* is a small fish resembling *kohada*. This fish is fermented with salt and vinegar. It is also used as a

*tane* for *nigiri*-zushi.
● *Ōmura*-Zushi **(Nagasaki)** This is a kind of *oshi*-zushi (pressed sushi) using not only fish and shellfish caught in the Bay of Omura but also vegetables.
● *Sake*-Zushi **(Kagoshima)** This is a sumptuous sushi made on spring festival days or to be eaten by those who have come to view the cherry blossoms. Rice is mixed with pink, sweet *sake* (rice wine), and fish, shellfish and vegetables are sandwiched between layers of sushi rice, with the top surface being decorated with an omelet thinly cut in thread-like pieces and boiled shrimp. It is weighed and allow to ferment for 5 to 6 hours.

# Glossary of Sushi

**Agari:** Tea, a special term used by sushi shops.

**Akami-dane:** Red-meat *tane*. Sushi-*dane* of red-meat fish, such as *toro* and *zuke* of tuna, and bonito meat.

**Chirashi-zushi:** Sushi rice in a bowl, with various eatables (*gu*) arranged on it. Also called *bara-zushi* in the Kansai District.

**Dashi:** Bonito fish stock, which is made by boiling bonito fish flakes and kelp. It is used as a base for various sushi ingredients and other Japanese cooking.

**Edomae:** A term used by sushi shops after World War II in Tokyo. *Edomae-zushi* is sushi using fish and shellfish caught in the Bay of Tokyo. The name, *Edomae-zushi*, still remains, but nowadays very few of the fish are taken from the bay.

**Funa-zushi:** A kind of sushi made in Shiga Prefecture. A kind of *nare-zushi*. It is said to be the oldest form of sushi in Japan, having a history of more than 1,000 years.

**Gari:** A special term used by sushi shops, meaning ginger seasoned with plain vinegar or sweetened vinegar. It is eaten to kill the aftertaste of sushi.

**Gu:** Ingredients for sushi and other Japanese cooking. Mainly eatables used as the core for *nori-maki* and *chirashi*-zushi. The word "*gu*" is never used for *nigiri*-zushi, for which the word *tane* is used.

**Gyoku:** Sushi-makers use this word for *Tamago-yaki* (omelet).

**Hako-zushi:** Box sushi. Also called Osaka-zushi. A kind of *Oshi*-zushi (pressed sushi), which is made by putting sushi ingredients and sushi rice in a box and by pressing the rice with both hands.

**Haya-zushi:** A kind of sushi which appeared about the middle of the 17th century. It was featured by a short fermentation period. It was made by adding table vinegar to rice and placing a heavy stone weight on it. *Nigiri*-zushi and *Hako*-zushi are kinds of *haya*-zushi.

**Hikari-mono:** Shining *tane*. Those of the fish meat sushi-*dane* which have a shining skin. Also called bluefish. *Hikari-mono* is usually used with the skin intact and after soaking in vinegar. Included among them are gizzard shad, halfbeak, and young sea bream.

**Kansai-zushi:** Osaka-zushi is to Osaka what *Edomae*-zushi is to Tokyo. A general term for sushi made in the kansai District, represented by *hako*-zushi, *bara*-zushi and *saba*-zushi.

**Kitsuke:** The slicing of fish and shellfish in forms suitable for use as *tane* for *nigiri*-zushi. Sushi-makers' word.

**Maki-mono:** A general term for sushi made by rolling sushi and *gu* with some ingredient, represented by *nori-maki*.

**Makisu:** Rolling bamboo mat. One of the sushi-making tools, which is used for making *maki-mono-zushi*. It is a screen-like mat.

**Mirin:** Sweet rice wine for cooking. Essential for seasoning sushi ingredients, *nikiri*, etc.

**Murasaki:** Sushi-makers' word for soy sauce.

**Nama-nari (-nare):** Lightly fermented sushi just before the appearance of *haya*-zushi. It appeared in the 15th century.

**Nare-zushi:** The oldest type of sushi, and the starting point of Japanese sushi. Sushi rice and fish were fermented fully for one to three years under a heavy stone weight. Only the fish was eaten, and the sushi rice was discarded. it is presently represented by *funa*-zushi.

**Nigiri-zushi:** Hand-formed sushi. A relatively new type of sushi, which was invented 160 to 170 years ago. This type of sushi has greatly changed the history of sushi, as sushi rice and *tane* came to be flavored by fermentation instantly by pressing them with both hands, in contrast to the fact that formerly sushi rice and ingredients had been fermented under a heavy stone weight. *Edomae*-zushi developed rapidly together with the appearance of *nigiri*-zushi.

**Nikiri:** Boiled soy sauce. Sushi-makers apply this sauce thinly to sushi before serving them to customers. *Mirin* is added to soy sauce at a ratio of 3 to 10, and is boiled for a short time.

**Nimono-dane:** Cooked or mainly boiled *tane*. Those of the fish and shellfish *tane* which are boiled before being used as *tane*. *Nitsume* is applied to them before they are served. Included among them are conger eel, mantis shrimp, etc.

**Nitsume:** Boiled-down conger eel broth. The broth that is applied to *nimono-dane*. Formerly, each different *tane* had *nitsume* made of the same *tane*. However, today conger eel broth is used for all kinds of *nimono-dane*.

**Nori:** Dried seaweed. One of the essential ingredients for sushi. Used for making *nori-maki* and *chirashi-zushi*.

**Nori-maki:** Sushi wound with seaweed. A representative *maki-mono zushi*. Toasted seaweed is used in Tokyo, but sushi-makers in the Kansai District use it without toasting it. They are called either *futo-maki* or *hoso-maki*, depending on whether they are made thick or thin. Furthermore, they are also called *kappa-maki*, *kampyo-maki*, and *tekka-maki*, according to the kinds of "*gu*" that is used.

**Oboro:** Whitefish flakes. A basic ingredient used for *chirashi*-zushi and others. It is sweet and looks pinkish in color.

**Sake:** Japanese rice wine. Also used as one of the basic seasonings. There is another "*sake*" meaning salmon.

**Sashimi:** Mainly very fresh raw fish and shellfish meat sliced in easy-to-eat forms. A representative Japanese dish. At sushi shops, it is served as a side dish (*tsumami*) for *sake*.

**Shiromi-dane:** White-meat *tane*. Whitefish meat *tane*, including sea bream, flounder and sea bass.

**Tamago-yaki:** Omelet. An essential ingredient for sushi. There are two kinds of omelet, a wafer-thin omelet and thick omelet. Sushi-makers' skill is tested by how well the omelet is cooked and seasoned.

**Tane (Dane) or Sushi-dane:** Sushi ingredients. A general term used mainly as toppings for *nigiri*-zushi. When it is preceded by a word, it is pronounced "*dane*".

**Te-zu:** Rice vinegar for wetting fingers and dampening the knife in sushi-making.

**Toro:** Sushi-makers' word for the fatty portion of tuna meat. One of the most popular sushi-*dane* today. There are two kinds of *toro*, *ō-toro* (very fatty) and *chū-toro* (slightly fatty).

**Tsuke:** Sushi-making work is generally called "*tsuke*". This is a remnant of the fact that in former days, the work of making sushi (*nare-zushi* and others) consisted of preserving or fermenting in vessels (*tsuke*). Thus, *tsuke-ba* means the kitchen of a sushi shop and *tsuke-dai* a cooking table.

**Tsuke-joyu:** Soy sauce in which sushi is dipped lightly just before it is eaten.

**Wasabi:** Japanese green horseradish. An absolutely necessary spice or condiment for sushi. There are two types: raw wasabi and powdered *wasabi*. The latter is made mainly of horseradish.

**Zuke:** The preliminary preparation of red-meat tuna by soaking it in soy sauce. This is expanded to mean red-meat tuna itself prepared in this way.

# Index    Names of Sushi and Sushi Ingredients